Braving Uncertainty

Braving Uncertainty

Maps for the Journey

Jim Ewing

First published in 2024 by:

Triarchy Press
Axminster, UK

www.triarchypress.net

ISBNs:
Print: 978-1-913743-89-5
eBook: 978-1-913743-90-1

tp

For Barbara

I was introduced to the maps and tools in this book over 10 years ago and I continue to find them extremely practical and useful for the small and large changes I have encountered. I have used them to plan and execute multi-year strategies as well as thinking through short term challenges growing a multinational business. I have also found them helpful when thinking through personal change. The tools reveal surprising insights and ideas to keep moving in uncertain times, they make it possible to understand what is holding us back and how to confront our fears when working at, and beyond, the edge of our comfort zone.

Eduardo Muñoz, CEO International Businesses, ME Elecmetal, Chile

I have used the tools described in this book to support bringing three very different teams together to create a single urgent care service. When things were tough and as a leadership team we were struggling to find hope, the Impacto framework really helped us to take stock and create shared common purpose. In the years leading up to this transformation work, much had been left unsaid, conflict had gnawed away between the different factions. Using the principles set out in TransforMAP and then the Implemento framework we managed to unlock conversations and get into shared, transformative action. All underpinned, of course, by good listening, hope and courage from the many members of the team.

Nickie Jakeman, NHS Accident & Emergency Consultant Physician, UK

Contents

Foreword

Many great stories have simple beginnings. I was introduced to Jim Ewing in 1989 as a work colleague who could help with a project I was tasked to deliver. We went on to transform the business we were working for; and then to change both our lives.

Jim started his career as an engineer in the satellite business and his curiosity about 'how things work' extended beyond circuits and 'thousand-mile-screwdrivers' to people and how they make their way in the world. He researched and experimented with a wide range of programmes and philosophies, exploring the conscious and subconscious, until his own special methodology emerged.

I observed Jim supporting a variety of people, in all sorts of places, and was regularly surprised when he took the conversation on an unexpected turn and produced a breakthrough. Jim's instinctive ability to ask the right question in changing circumstances was masterful – guided by his belief that navigating change is navigating life.

Over time he documented his approach in simple maps to provide direction for others on this journey. The successful application of these keeps us busy as Executive Arts, supporting, consulting and coaching individuals and organisations as they design, innovate and learn their way through change.

Unfortunately, we can no longer call on Jim for guidance so, with the editorial help of Graham Leicester of International Futures Forum, we offer this book which pulls together Jim's thinking, writing, artwork and instruction. It's a reflective and practical resource for our times – a supplement to your own skills and practice, helping to move your thinking forward, often in remarkable ways.

Throughout Jim's life he was fascinated by people and their stories. His journey was a great one. We invite you, with the support of Jim's maps, to navigate your own.

Patrick Heneghan

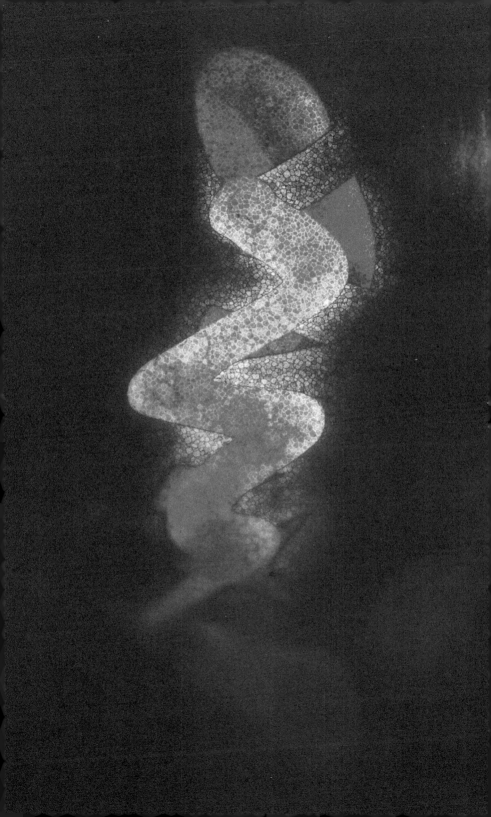

Braving Uncertainty

We have to trust the invisible gauges we carry within. We have to realise that a creative being lives within ourselves, whether we like it or not, and that we must get out of its way, for it will give us no peace until we do.
From *Centering* by Mary Caroline Richards

For thirty years and more I have spent my professional life with people living at the learning edge. Individuals, teams, groups, companies, organisations.

They are moved to this point, to the threshold of change, loss and possibility, by any number of things: by circumstance, by events, by upheaval, by the inevitable surprises and transitions that are part of life. Or they are feeling the call and the stirring of their 'creative being' demanding attention, as M.C. Richards puts it, and can ignore it no longer.

I have developed a practice for supporting people in this place to brave the uncertainty of transition and change, to help them let go of what is past and no longer serving their purpose and to embrace a more fulfilling future. They need to change their minds, their choices and the stories they tell themselves. With the minimum of fuss.

Over time this approach has fed a distinctive and successful consulting practice for myself and a small number of colleagues, working mostly with companies going through change and more recently with the public and social sectors dealing with increasingly 'wicked' problems.

This book is intended to share our learning with a much wider community. The early chapters reflect on the overall approach and its origins in both theory and practice. The latter part shares a family of frameworks or maps for transformative conversations that have emerged from the work.

I hope the material here will provide just enough scaffolding to encourage you down this path. The final chapter points to other resources for follow-up and support.

Origins

I started my professional life in the 1960s as a rocket scientist at TRW, a US aerospace company, helping to design spacecraft. It was there that my boss spotted that meetings in the company seemed to go better when I was in the room. They sent me to school to develop what they saw as a talent for getting the best out of people facing change.

That was the start of a learning journey. A dozen years later I left the company, determined to pursue my curiosity about people further. Something drew me to up sticks and move a hundred miles away to California where in the 1970s I started to immerse myself in all the edgy, revolutionary therapies that time and that place had to offer – Transactional Analysis, Gestalt Therapy, Psychodrama, Voice Dialogue, you name it.

I was blessed with good teachers and willing subjects to practice on. I was passionately bidding for the knowledge and the powers to help others best navigate change, to create transformative vision, and to make flawless choices when there was never enough information.

I was searching for a conversational, casual, no-frills and no-waiting intervention to be a first responder for individuals and for groups when steep change and life redesign come calling.

I wanted to develop, as consciously as possible, a way to support others who are out on that precipice where emerging talent and vision meet uncertainty, fear and wide-open possibility. I call that the 'learning edge'.

It is a life-giving path that leads us to our learning edge. I realised over time that it is an amazing engine of growth, development and becoming. There our actions are guided not only by our rational minds but also by emergent patterns and inner stirrings, unconscious knowledge, dreams, hunches, urges, mysteries, unsettledness and nagging, enigmatic questions, slips of the tongue, symptoms of illness and wellness, resistance, avoidance, gambits, teases, surprises.

There, if we pay attention, we can engage our latent talents clamouring to get on stage. We can renegotiate everything. We can make wiser choices, live out renewed, more compelling stories, and be more than we ever thought we could be.

The Learning Edge

My work is based on engendering a creative relationship with unknowing. When we are skilled at exploring uncertain spaces and finding meaning and direction and learning there, we are better able to handle the uncertainties when the world pulls the rug from under us.

I started to see that at our learning edge, one foot anchors us in the rational light of what we believe we know. The other foot probes the dark beyond the edge, into the unknown, the unfathomable vastness of life. The creative tension between these two spaces brings our learning edge alive.

To keep our balance at this edge is like riding a bicycle. On a bike we are always in danger of falling over, pedalling forward to give enough velocity to steer the bike underneath us and keep it upright. We are balanced only when we are in motion. So it is in our lives.

In my experience, those who seem to be able to handle this uncertainty of learning, of innovation, of staying, of leaving, and all the rest, and carry on with enduring faith in realising their purposes in life, share a couple of things.

First, and absolutely required, they are clear about their strengths. They trust them. They are always in the equation. These powers will be used over and over in our lives. They are our birthright. They will be put to work in different contexts and ages and manners. They give us our fundamental life in the world.

People who are comfortable at the learning edge are always consciously aware of their strongest abilities, their powers, talents and skills. They will not sacrifice those for anyone or any situation.

Second, they understand that beyond the edge lies the unknown. Whatever new they are experimenting with is just that, an experiment, a learning journey, a pursuit of discovery which will produce a wide set of novel conditions. Some conditions will build on, amplify, and provide contrast and depth to their core strengths. Other conditions will seem to diminish or de-energise the core and call forth other capacities so far hidden or denied.

Part of balancing at the edge involves calling on all of our faculties, our ways of knowing and being. It is a challenge, for example, to really desire something from our hearts and yet stay conscious enough actually to evaluate in a disciplined way the range of conditions which then arise and which need to be navigated in order to realise our desire. People who handle the learning edge well do both. Their hearts and bodies give clues for pushing into the mists, while their minds remain engaged, making considered choices not merely determined by the heart.

Sometimes we may wobble, or worse. Everything tells us that turning the bike or pedalling harder will bring us upright. But we did not see the patch of oil on the ground and we fall on our head. It happens. Does that bring into question our value to the world? Should we doubt our capacity to ride a bike? Should we give up trying? Should we draw back from the learning edge? Or do we learn to see more capably, to find more in every moment to notice and be aware of and to feed our purposes?

In practice we live at the learning edge all the time – even if we sometimes need to be called up short, shaken awake, to realise it. Navigating upheaval, disruption, renewal and redesign are a required course in this life. Stuff happens – and when it does our minds will be changed, along with our choices and the stories we tell ourselves of who we are and where we are headed. This is truly challenging work.

When healthy people choose to experience change as a dark, scary drama, or a pathology or sickness to be gotten over, they waste angst, time and resources, with victimhood, bad feelings and sub-optimal choices thrown into the bargain. This dark view of change is a heritage of Western culture.

My work transforms this cultural assumption and habit. For me the inner journey to make an authentic transformation is identical with the journey of the designer, the artist and the learner.

Authentic design, innovation, learning and transition, at their core, are much the same. Something outworn or unavailable from the past is left behind, abandoned. Something valuable, also from the past, is reframed, re-imagined, and re-contexted to serve us again, in a new manner.

Uncertainty is a constant companion. Exploration, experiments, and imagining based on inklings, nudges, inspirations and passions sketch out a direction. Bets are placed, and choices taken guided by pragmatic, informed hope.

If we are fortunate, and chance does play a role in this, we can see a bit more clearly, we are at one with the world, aligned within ourselves and making some headway on our deeper purposes for being in this life.

The artist and designer can cultivate a creative relationship with unknowing in this way. We will not know the outcomes when we begin. We may not even know what we are working toward. Even the time required is not predictable, taking moments or months.

Every tool I have developed over the years leads us to this learning edge. For me, it is a discovery place I look forward to entering, where we can find meaning, direction and learning and genuinely create better choices out of uncertainty. It is an environment I find I can create with another person at virtually no cost. It is a place of high play.

At the learning edge we discover that a deep, inner wisdom about what is right for us, now, is always somewhere within us.

Maps for the Journey

I have spent a lifetime supporting people dealing with change and uncertainty at their learning edge. I listen for signals, encourage expansive transition, construct stories, tease coherence from the mess.

I noticed that over years of collaboration, study, design and practice, recurring patterns of inquiry and procedure emerged, both with individuals and in groups. I developed ways of making these patterns and processes accessible to others by creating a family of maps of the territory. These maps are designed to bring the many contradictory human responses triggered by change and uncertainty to the surface for examination: the forces of excitement and resistance, clarity and confusion, hope and despair which, more or less consciously, are inevitably aroused when we encounter or even contemplate the unknown.

This is the critical work, raising awareness in ourselves and others of the forces in play in the human system. But it is only part of the story of change and transformation. We must also acknowledge the context we are operating in and the situation we face, the external forces at work beyond our inner worlds, and the skills and knowledge we bring to the design of the steps we decide to take to address our predicament. The maps guide those processes too.

The core suite consists of five maps – Insight Cycle, Stucco, Implemento, Impacto and TransforMAP. Together they offer a range of ways to create pathways to clear thinking, enabling relationships and more effective action for individuals, groups, communities and organisations.

TransforMAP was one of the earliest maps I developed, a map of the territory of a changing mind, changing choices and a changing story. It helps us document where things stand so we get an idea of where we are in the process. Used dynamically for inquiry and reflection, the experience moves us along. Completing the past, mapping out possibility and the learning to be done, and framing the story of change at a human, personal level. In other words, it enables a reading of the landscape of change that embraces the sub-conscious aspects of life. It revolves around three 'voices' triggered by change: a voice of endings full of fear and angst, a voice of reinvention full of energy and exploration, and a voice of commitment full of discipline and intention.

Given its foundational status, I have included an appendix telling the story of how the TransforMAP was developed, including details of other reading on the sources underpinning my own learning for those who want to go deeper.

More recently, the Insight Cycle has provided the principal entry point to my work. If you take the TransforMAP as offering access to the interior conversation at the learning edge, then the Insight Cycle maps the exterior manifestation, the external drivers for the internal struggle. What's happening in our head, and what's happening outside our head. The Insight Cycle offers access to assumptions and worldviews which are inside our head. But it gets there by looking at what we are acting out in the world. These maps are overlays. Start with either one and then do the other, and back again.

The other maps – Stucco, Implemento and Impacto –– all relate to and pick up on specific aspects of these main maps. Stucco explores the voice of endings, the sense of being stuck. Implemento explores the voice of reinvention, and the design of new initiatives. Impacto explores the voice of commitment, and how to engage others in our chosen endeavours.

These maps help to frame transformative conversations. They act both as guides to a conversation and places to record what is said. Together they offer a range of ways to create pathways to clear thinking, productive relationships and more effective action. They will enable anyone with a suitable conversational craft to work with others to resolve transitional problems right away, make better choices and live better stories.

In the second part of this book I introduce each map in turn, explaining and describing what they depict and how they can be used in practice. Treat those chapters as an introduction, enough to grasp the fundamentals. The maps will work straight out of the box, without need for extensive background reading. They are designed to be as simple and intuitive as possible, to draw people to the learning edge. Equally, as with any practice, additional guidance and support can be helpful. The final chapter suggests the path ahead, starting with my friends and colleagues at Executive Arts who continue to practise, codify, share and develop this work.

In any event, as the initial chapters that follow make clear, to get the best out of these maps and frameworks it helps to understand some of the thinking that lies behind them and to understand that there is a conversational craft to be learned as well. That craft rests on practices of open listening and fair storymaking.

These are key to the possibility of accessing and paying attention to otherwise unconscious knowledge, both in ourselves and in the universe. Each one of the maps is designed to tap into that usually hidden resource. Each has some kind of 'trick' or sleight of hand to encourage us to express out loud things we did not know we knew or perhaps feel too uncomfortable to acknowledge.

Successful application is not just about mastering the tools and the procedures for their use. It is the quality of our being and our being with, our presence, that will bring these maps and conversational practices to life.

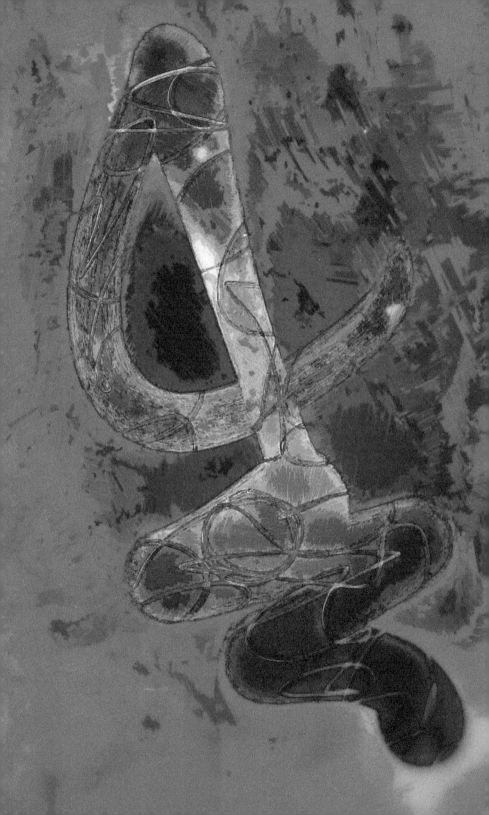

Change and Transition

If we are to become skilled in revealing a different story about change and uncertainty, as a design opportunity rather than a dark foreboding, then we must gain a better understanding of change itself – where it comes from and how we typically respond.

The forces of change are both external and internal, and the two are tightly linked. Operating well at the learning edge is about both having the courage to initiate a step into the unknown and the awareness to know when the external environment or our own inner stirrings demand it.

We tend to think of change as adaptation – a response to the changing exterior landscape. That's important. Reading that landscape and understanding the forces in play is an ability that is fundamental to the success of individuals, communities, businesses and organisations in the modern world. But to be effective we also need to learn to work with our inevitable responses and reactions to change – the inner dimensions – in a positive way.

It is normal for change – or even the prospect of change – to generate a reaction, be it physical or psychological. We all react to change, consciously and unconsciously, and we are all different. Some like change. They thrive on new ideas and challenges. Others don't. They thrive on stability and familiarity. Some of us like the curves while others like the straights, and much of the time which we prefer depends on the context and the circumstances.

Many of our physical systems are designed to work against change. In our bodies, for example, the main function of the hypothalamus is homeostasis – maintaining the body's status quo. Factors such as blood pressure, body temperature, fluid and electrolyte balance, and body weight are held to a precise value called the set point. Although this set point can migrate over time, from day to day it is remarkably fixed.

To achieve this, the hypothalamus must receive inputs about the state of the body and must be able to initiate compensatory changes if anything shifts off balance. These natural physiological processes lie deep within us, usually unnoticed.

Sometimes the external environment changes dramatically and the body fails to cope. Then we notice. For survival, the rate of change in an organism must equal or exceed the rate of change in the environment in which it exists. For that reason, much 'adaptation' in practice involves escape – moving to a different environment.

Transition and Surprise

At a personal level, many of the significant changes we face in our lives can be anticipated. They are inevitable transitions. Shakespeare was not the first to recognise 'seven ages'. All the great spiritual traditions suggest some pattern of development over time. For as long as animals have existed, we have aged and staged.

We awake, alive, soaking up experience through our first years. Puberty strikes. We leave childhood for responsibility. We connect, partner, career, parent and then wake up one day and realise we are halfway through our life and wonder who we really are and what we really want to be doing with the time left. Not to mention who that person is sleeping next to us in the bed. The light changes, from morning to afternoon, as Jung suggested, and we leave youth behind and engage our mid-lives and then our older lives and then the final times.

Moving through the stages takes resources and work to learn, innovate and redesign, to make the transition from one set of circumstances to another. Each shift requires a change in the story of who we are, the choices we therefore make and the development of a wider set of assumptions, values and beliefs to deal with our wider life.

Some of us get stuck for a while. Even for years and years. Some try to jump stages. Some resist and avoid and fight the natural flow. The big one, our death, will not be avoided, no matter how we may try. One of my favourite quips is that in America death is assumed to be optional.

Natural, age- and stage-driven changes usually give us plenty of time to accomplish each transition. But a big external shock to the system, like a devastating flood, an economic recession, or the diagnosis of a serious illness, moves us into another realm, another context of transformation. I call these the 'wicked forces'.

Wicked forces arrive, unbidden, without warning, or with plenty of ignored or denied signs and portents. And then, in a moment, wham, we are slammed by an unavoidable upheaval.

The organisation no longer needs our expertise. The company fails. The world experiences dislocations and change at unprecedented scale. Gun-slinging sociopaths and psychopaths take positions of power. The climate effects of burning massive amounts of carbon for our comfort and holidays in Barcelona come home to roost. The doctor has some bad news.

Wicked forces are bigger than any one of us. Bigger than our tribes and communities. No one is in charge. If there is any control, it is in the shadows. Usually things happen so fast there is not enough time to make the discoveries, learnings and adjustments for a graceful transition. Or the diagnosis comes out of a clear blue sky, with no warning and no rational explanation. There is shock, dislocation, disruption and we are faced with rebooting our lives.

Coherence and Story

Being able to make sense of our lives, giving them meaning and coherence, is a fundamental human necessity. The transitions and surprises we all encounter in life must somehow be incorporated into our existing frameworks. This is the inner work of change – adapting the story we tell ourselves to make sense of who we are, where we are going and how the world is going to support us in the journey.

Satisfactory changes cause us to grow, to use more of ourselves, to extend our being into added dimensions. Unsatisfying changes are frauds, because we just repeat the same old life patterns in a different guise. And, for all the money spent and the effort put forth, we receive the same old life outcomes.

The growth response requires the release and restructuring of established life patterns. We evolve ourselves by shedding old patterns, expanding our self-definition and identity, evolving new life methods and relationships and re-patterning our lives around them.

That means changing our story. That story is constructed from the material we find in our inner world: questions, dreams, angst, confusion, determination, excuses, powers, limits, worldviews, beliefs, assumptions, values. It also draws on our experience of the outer world: forces, possibilities, risks and influences, campaigns, teams, dramas, wins, losses, battles and so on.

We all carry, at least unconsciously, some such narrative of our lives covering both inner and outer worlds, telling what for us feels like the whole picture. If it is extracted from us in the telling it is likely to be a coherent, emotional and action-based story, made up inside the boundaries of what we believe we know about our past, our dreams for the future and the powers, limits, possibilities and risks we presently imagine to be working for or against us.

The story is a construction of our mind, a thought piece, disconnected from direct experience but drawing from it, crafted to minimise the need for significant change and to maintain an uninterrupted flow of our preferred pleasures of life. This is our cover story which justifies our life's predicament.

To make this story hang together and remain limited to our knowing, it will have logical disconnects throughout, missing chapters, twists in the interpretation of past events to make them fit, questionable assumptions about other people's motives and a worldview which may not withstand too much scrutiny.

An upbeat, optimistic version of our story may describe a grand adventure – a challenging, invigorating mountain or two to be climbed. That kind of encouraging life story naturally prompts further elaborate plans and strategies for the future for the highest accomplishment.

A downbeat, discouraging story likely holds failure, unsustainable living or working, the loss of a loved one, overwhelming disruption, or a nasty turn of fortune. This discouraging story begs for answers to reduce the pain.

The division is never as clearly drawn as this, up or down, triumph or disaster. Our story at any time is more likely to be a jumble of both.

In the face of significant shocks to the system, wicked forces, the story we tell ourselves, structured to minimise disruption and pain and to preserve pleasure in life, runs into inexplicable trouble. Something beyond the limits of our comfortable world has pulled the rug out from under us.

The temptation is to 'fix' the cover story, patch it up with more of the same material, inside the bounds of what we know we know. But that's what has left the story wanting to start with. Fixing continues an illusion of control and predictability – a cover story crafted to keep the enduring and pervasive uncertainty of life out of our view and experience. A disturbance in the system can be the opportunity for growth and realignment. Fixing, on the other hand, disconnects from much of what our insight might bring to the conversation, erasing the opportunity to discover more foundational truths in our lives.

We are at the learning edge. The upheavals are greater than our story can handle and there are no answers within the boundaries of our existing assumptions. Some larger chaos is afoot: forces unseen, mysterious, incognito, stirring the pot, making trouble, just as they also offer wider possibilities.

Embracing the Mess

Such is the unfathomable universal mystery, which I call the natural Mess, of which we are a living part. We are inseparable from it by any linguistic or symbolic trick played in our heads. Our made-up personal cover story is what we use to split our awareness of what is going on in the world in two. We attempt to live in the made-up version, so we don't have continually to confront the uncertain upheavals of the moment-to-moment fluid dance of all things of which we are also aware, deep down. As T.S. Eliot said, 'Humankind cannot bear very much reality'.

This fiction is necessary in the short term to get things done. But if we forget that we have made up this story and start believing it as true and sacrosanct, we make far more pain and suffering for ourselves than letting go of the pattern when its usefulness has run out and exploring the resources that this freedom releases.

The natural Mess is ever changing, beyond control or influence, beyond anything we can ever hope to fully understand. We can feel it at work. We can experience things coming our way through it and just as surely being taken away by it. It brings moments of immense clarity as surely as it raises unfathomable questions.

We each belong to the natural Mess as it belongs to us. We are deeply influenced by it. Deeply influenced in the dimensions of ourselves which lie outside of waking awareness. We rarely if ever see these dimensions directly. We see their effect on our daily lives. And we make up stories to explain what is going on, to keep ourselves 'grounded' and separate from the unfathomable.

Try as we might, we cannot really separate from our life as part of this larger Mess. The huge array of our being, stretching beyond our conscious selves, the waking, thinking, consciousness we refer to as 'I', is in the dance all the time. And all the time it has is the present moment. In the Mess there is no past and no future – those are mental constructs our conscious mind uses for our convenience.

Our whole body-mind is in this ever-changing dance. Our conscious self denies the dance in favour of predictability and control, setting up a conflict within. When changes come with so much upheaval and disruption that our conscious self can no longer maintain the illusion of stability, the logical story fails and we are thrown back into that which we tried to deny, the Mess, where our lives are constantly changing and constantly uncertain.

This tension between the logical sense we try to impose on our lives and any felt sense of disturbance or disruption will almost always show up first as a question. We each carry life questions which surface from time to time: Who am I? What will become of me? Should I do this work or that? Choose this relationship, move to that city, become a parent, intervene or not in my kids' lives? And so on.

These are enigmatic questions which lead us not to straight-forward yes or no answers, but to more compelling inquiries. Without clear answers, we must make do with hunches, pathfinding, and learning through action, with one foot in what we think we know and one in an unseen which unfolds as we go along.

It helps to love a good mystery and have a personal tolerance for pushing on without being at all sure of our footing. When there are no answers, the enigma that lies behind the questions becomes our guiding star. The pursuit of these questions, seeing into and through them, is the work to be done, carrying us on until the unseen resolves out of the mists into more pragmatic purposes and plans.

When individuals, families, teams, organisations and communities experience an upheaval, a disruption, or a spike in uncertainty, the unanswerable questions arise and come to the fore. They may present initially as a jam, a dilemma, a conundrum or otherwise. At the root is an enigma and a set of unanswerable questions to be revealed, explored and more deeply understood.

Expansive Change

The required depth of understanding will come from drawing on all that we know and all our ways of knowing. Most obviously, we carry a rich store of life answers within us at all times, constructed from our past experience. Our conscious mind has plenty of experience in gaining direct access to this area of our body's memory system.

At the same time, a profound set of guideposts to more expansive change also lies within us. Deep in our body-mind, usually removed from direct conscious access, we know which outworn patterns to let go and what new quality of being we are ready to express. Whether external life circumstances drive us to change or whether we are moved to do so through inner stirrings and unease, we have the direction we need, within ourselves. These guideposts remain outside of our conscious access until we learn to locate them and draw them out.

When we begin to experience confusing and unexpected physical, emotional or perceptual symptoms, these are, in my view, signals of the need for an expansive change. They signal to us that the way things are no longer tallies with the way things were. Something doesn't feel right. These symptoms are also effective doorways to our inner wisdom.

Such symptoms include non-ordinary things we notice about ourselves and our relationship with our environment. An intrigue with a new person or project might be such a symptom. So might a brief, unexpected downtime, a nightmare, a daydream or a vision, as well as the range of temporary physical sensations and even chronic conditions we experience. If we become aware of a change in our condition, whether we judge it better or worse, we are perceiving a potential symptom of expansive change.

Most of us, mistakenly, view these symptoms as the direct cause of our joy or frustration. Our resulting actions, based on this mistaken assumption, tend simply to address the symptoms and rarely bring the life success we seek.

For example, if I am a busy, urban adult and a symptom appears to impede my life's activity, I will usually seek immediate symptomatic relief rather than examine underlying causes. I don't seem to have enough time for the things I really care about: I go on a time management programme.

If the symptom seems to enhance my experience, I am also likely to address it only at face value and attempt to intensify and guarantee its recurrence. I start going to the gym and find that I enjoy working out. Clearly I need to do this more often, perhaps six times a week – and possibly enter an Iron Man contest.

Most of us throw away our symptoms in this way and miss their full life enhancing potential. To me these are not just surface symptoms but indicators of inner conflict, the links to inner wisdom and creative, present living. From this perspective we may proceed to very different conclusions about what our symptom is revealing to us and what is to be done about it. We may reduce our emphasis on attending to symptoms and increase our sense of personal integrity and inner satisfaction.

This brings us to one fundamental strategy for recognising and moving through an expansive change. We are healthier when we can sense the stirrings of change early on. Listening to the symptoms and noticing the signals they are sending us, we can locate our inner wisdom and, by applying it to our network of relationships, update our pattern of life.

This view suggests a healthy balance between spiritual, mental, physical and social activities. Expansive change occurs on all levels, from the farthest reaches of our Higher Self, if you will, through our patterns of conscious mentation and emotional patterns of relationship, to the most mundane physical patterns of body movement. We start to look, feel, think, even move, differently.

Expansive change does not rely on one level more than another. It is not more spiritual than it is physical or vice versa. It is not necessarily more mental than emotional, nor does it require specific relational shifts more than inner re-patterning. It is all of the above, in some balance which uniquely suits the individual.

Through my work with individuals in transition, I've noticed some essential life skills for those who create successful and relatively distress-free expansive transitions. These skills can be observed equally in groups or organisations in transition:

- They use intriguing symptoms that they notice as guidance for the release of established patterns and the starting place for designing new ones
- They open a new chapter in their life dream to allow a re-patterning to occur
- They revalue, forgive, heal and release past experience and learning
- They negotiate changes in their personal network of relationships to reflect and nourish the re-patterning
- They establish a supportive daily discipline during the transition process.

There is one final shared attribute – again evident in individuals, groups and organisations. They tend to be able to locate fellow travellers and guides, one or more reasonably neutral, healthy individuals who can be 'present' with them during this expansive period, a source of psychological safety. That is the subject of the next chapter.

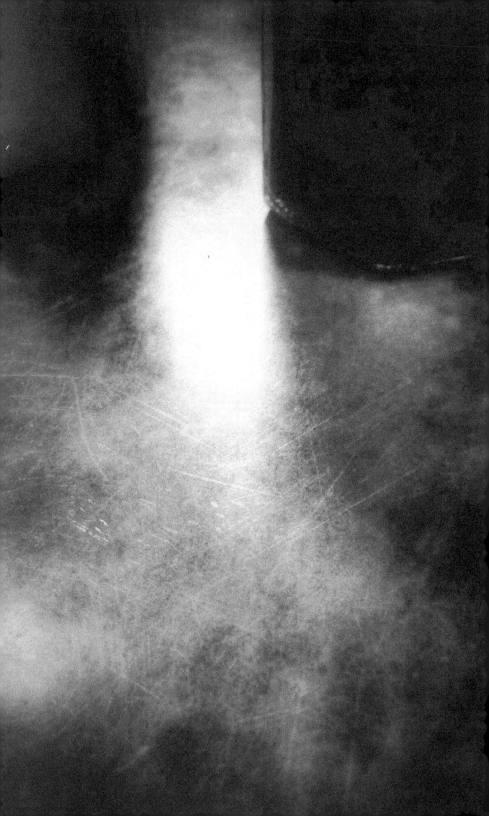

Supporting Transition

It is hard to embrace change alone – either change forced upon us or change willingly undertaken in pursuit of growth and development. We need a pattern of supportive relationship. No solo climbers.

If we aspire to be on the end of a rope for an individual or a group going through expansive change, we need to ask what kind of support people need at the learning edge 'out on that precipice where emerging talent and vision meet uncertainty, fear and wide-open possibility'?

Transformative Presence

We might assume that the answer to this question involves some sort of 'help'. On close examination, however, the definitions of the word 'help' do not entirely serve those in the process of re-patterning their lives. The definitions tend towards treatment and move into the prevention and removal of things. This is appropriate if a symptom is so acute that essential life support activity is in jeopardy.

Usually, however, people are not in immediate danger. Therefore, assuming the symptoms they are starting to notice hold a useful signal about new directions and actions, being 'helped' may well remove the signal and, with it, their ability to perceive the message and to proceed more effectively into expansive change.

What we seem to need most during a transition is not 'help' as such but someone to be present, to be an attentive 'presence'. We need the presence of another neutral person who is in a relatively stable, healthy life space and who has ideally themselves experienced at least one major transition associated with becoming their own person. Someone who will be there, with whom we can share our predicament and our vision.

We could also reasonably ask for someone who has maps

of the territory we will be travelling, with references should we require them, and tools to help sense our place and direction, build our dreams, release the past and renew our support networks for the future.

You may wish to take on this support role yourself, or you may be called upon to do so. Whatever maps and processes, tools and frameworks we bring to bear in these circumstances, ultimately the success of our work will rest on our capacity, as guides, to enter an uncertain space, dedicated to the well-being of another, putting our creative capacities in their service, rather than our own. I dare say there is some falling in love to be done. Love in the sense of being completely curious and interested in all the ins and outs of the person(s) across the table. Not that we don't learn too. A genuinely big conversation serves all of us. But this is the frosting on the cake, not our first agenda.

I suggest there are three fundamental levels in the inquiries we pursue with those we seek to support at the learning edge.

The first level is problem-solving. At this point we might show up as an expert offering answers. A tax accountant knows which forms are required, what goes in what boxes and when and how it gets submitted to the tax office. The doctor hears that I have a headache, assesses the sensations I report and prescribes a useful medicine. A cleric with deep knowledge of which verses are to be studied and prayers to be made has ready answers which satisfy the follower.

Such expert answer-giving is the very bottom of the transformative scale of things. No harm and no foul here. This is where most of us start out and most continue developing over the length of a career. Providing answers pays pretty well and is a valued and immediate path to a successful transaction. If the client needs an answer and their question is limited and clear enough and we think we have a useful solution, we will not likely keep it from them.

However, when upheaval strikes, fast answers may seem filling, like fast food, but do not provide genuine nourishment. We are then called to engage in realms where the outcomes cannot be known at the outset and navigating the unanswerable is our work.

This second level is transformative inquiry. In these circumstances people often present a question relating to choice. There are too many choices. There are no choices. A choice has been taken. It seems risky and uncertain. It's a done deal, now what? Or a question of procedure: how do I bring my teenage daughter around to my sense of what she needs to do with her time?

As guides, we are torn a bit here. We can fall back into expert advice based on past experience. I assure you that advice will not be useful. We cannot know enough about another person's experience to deliver advice. We have our own mind model of who he or she is. That is not them, it is us. We can pretend and tell ourselves we are really good at advice. Such hubris is simply delusional.

Change-driven times hold elements of the new and unseen which risk making advice based on past experience out of date, inappropriate, misplaced and unhelpful. That said, getting all the advice out of our system by writing it down in a private notebook is a fine discipline. It gets it out of us, gets it witnessed by ourselves. With it out, we are not as likely to offer it later.

Then we can embark on an exploration which will wind up in wise initiative, but of a type and from a place we cannot predict when we begin. This is transformative inquiry. The work is of the client and for the client. The good news is we don't have to be experts at all. We just pursue artful conversations and guide others into helpful frameworks of thinking. Mastering such processes prepares us to converse easily from the transformative, learning edge viewpoint, without any tools on the table.

The third level is presence. This is the very top of the heap – the heat of the night, if you will. The job has evaporated. The loved one is lost to the mysteries of a death. Health and all future assumptions and plans vanish in a three-minute message from the doctor. Our client is deep in the middle of disruption and uncertainties and there is really nothing to be said and nothing to be done. Every one of us is taken by these forces some time in our existence.

These are not Hallmark Card moments. Platitudes and feel-good slogans are completely unhelpful. We need the art of high attendance, attending to another from the broadest perspective of life, death and the mysteries of human existence. This is the most challenging work to master.

While we appear to be sitting with the other person and doing pretty much nothing, there is much going on under the surface. We are an affirming presence. We are 'there' in the largest and deepest sense of the word. We hold a big, non-judgemental open space for the other to be whoever they need to be at the time. There is nothing to be done, so we show up as a wise and thoughtful witness. We just sit in the exquisite moments when someone confronts their core. Being a transformative presence is the highest form of our art – a goal that must from the outset inform all our practice.

Open Listening

Let us step back for now from this high plateau to the middle ground of transformative inquiry. This is fundamentally a conversational practice.

As we know, change, innovation and learning are riddled with uncertainty and disruption. We tend to react with fear, unpleasant feelings and an urge to avoid the whole mess. While some of our natural responses are very useful, much of this negative feeling and angst wastes our time in lostness, confusion, uncertainty, fears and doubts.

In transformative inquiry, our first job is to help clear out that waste, and harvest the wisdom buried in the good stuff. This frees up great energy. Our second job puts that energy to work finding a right path out of the mess. We change the perspective from fear, loss and avoidance to letting go of the past, building possibility and making a commitment to a transformed outcome, which we cannot see at the start of our journey. The route to such insight is very simple: we must give people a damned good listening to.

How many times in your life have you had someone who is at least half sane and smart really listen to you? Make space for whatever you had to say? Make notes and share them without judgement or psycho-emotional baggage, and stay with it until you had really said all there was to say?

The chances are you have never had that luxury. We don't prepare teachers, parents, coaches, the clergy or doctors to do this kind of work. It takes too long, making it seem economically inefficient in a culture which makes money on cookie cutter efficiency.

This is about listening without judgement or prejudice. Focusing on what people say rather than what you ask them. Listening until they are repeating themselves – exhaustive listening. Capturing everything as you go.

Invite the person in front of you to tell you more about whatever part of their lives they seem to want to share. Make visible notes so they know they have been heard. Let them correct the notes as they go, to keep yourself from over-interpreting what they say.

The quality of your listening will also be a function of your contribution to the conversation, your promptings and your questions. Most listening is really based on what the listener wants, not what the subject has to explore. So most of the time we are asked closed questions – those that have a ready 'yes' or 'no' answer. In the worst case, we feel interrogated. Much of the time we are asked leading questions to find the guilty party. Or at least to elicit answers the questioner wants to hear.

Contrast that with the gentle conversational partner who explores with open questions, listening thoroughly and inviting more. Even sharing some things of him or herself. The likely result is a surprise discovery, some trust, some appreciation of each other's predicament.

Open listening is based on an invitation to explore and express something. Wherever the person you are working with goes with that invitation, we go too. We invite someone to tell us about the future they see for themselves. If they start talking about some past experience that brings them down, we track that. We do not come back and remind them of our question and insist they respond to that specifically. The story emerges in the telling and the quality of our listening encourages the speaker to surprise themselves with the barely conscious knowledge that comes to the surface.

The highest compliment I ever got for my work was that I was 'tracing' the other person. Right with them. Not ahead or behind. Exactly there, tuned in on some ideal wavelength to who they were in the moment.

Fair Storymaking

There may also be an aspect of sense-making in our listening. I call this 'fair storymaking'.

People going through change are in the process of changing stories. We can act as a catalyst for that process by finding plausible structure, meaning and coherence in what we hear. We can put it all together in some way that adds value to the conversation. It enriches the space we are holding with the person. We learn more. The speaker learns more.

If we do try to tell their story we must do so in a way that they can hear without any of the sense of assault or violation or over-interpretation or resistance which almost always comes with feedback, no matter how friendly.

Why is feedback usually quite hard to take? It is most often the first word of the sentence that does it. "You ..." As soon as I start talking about you, using that pronoun, two things happen.

First, I have in practice separated myself from you. I am no longer with you. I am the observer and you are the observed. Second, the word "You" has a finger pointed at you implied in there. We all grew up with parents and teachers correcting us. They were the parents and we were the kids. We never forget that feeling of being pointed at, usually with some sort of criticism or embarrassment or guilt-making stuff flowing into us. And we all learned how to shut it out, because it was painful.

If we begin by observing what "you" are, what you are doing, saying and, heaven help us, what you are feeling, we have lost the person we have been exhaustively and openly listening to at the first line. They put up the blast shields and rapport is a distant memory.

What to do instead? First the separation issue, which is really my problem. I have to stay with you. So, the simplest thing to do is just become you. It's a role play where I use what I have learned about my partner to act as if I were her. All I have to do is say, "I am Harriet". And then be the Harriet in myself who has formed by the intense listening and tracing and notemaking I have done.

From here on I use the first person pronoun 'I'. "I am a person who..." and see what comes out. "I am a person who is becoming..." "I am a person who once..." "I am a person who aspires to..." I'm just being the Harriet I have heard and trusting that something useful will come through me that the Harriet sitting across from me can use. This may feel strange for some, so it is always worth checking in after a couple of minutes and asking "How is this for you?". If you get a nod, keep going. If not, ask instead how they would like you to help.

This approach also addresses the second problem of raising Harriet's blast shields. I haven't used 'you' at all. In fact, from Harriet's view I am really talking about myself. "I am a person who..." is in some way about me, not Harriet. At least that's what the internal defender among Harriet's sub-personalities experiences. So the blast shields remain down and whatever I say can be taken on board.

The third part of this, which works with both the separation and resistance problem and helps me and Harriet immensely, is that I do not make any eye contact.

If I do, I'll be looking for cues from her about how I'm doing. That is fatal. The whole setup falls apart in an instant. I am in my head thinking about what I'm doing and, in my body-mind, subconsciously adapting my story for approval. I lose the sublime connection with her.

So, I forge ahead and worry not about how I'm doing. I know how I'm doing. I'm fully being Harriet. I notice different figures of speech than I would usually use myself. New ideas. Harriet speaks new things she never said out loud through me. I'm some sort of conduit for her. I have no internal baggage to limit what I say whilst being Harriet. She gets a version of herself full on.

When I feel I'm done, then I make eye contact and the first thing that comes out of my mouth is a simple question, "How am I doing?" Rest with that and listen to Harriet. No explaining, no softening or apologies. Just stop, ask the question and shut up.

The Insight Cycle

People and their organisations come into existence, go through stages of growth, periods of good health and bad, times of relative calm and predictability and other times of intense turbulence, chaos and uncertainty. Every organisation and every person gets born, grows, gets stuck and lost and off path, learns, gains, loses, finds new ways, develops knowledge and wisdom and comes to an end. Such are the cycles of becoming on the paths we live out. Every day, as individuals or organisations, we create this journey. We are continually becoming.

Individuals want to have insight, live out stimulating intentions, find wisdom, compete successfully, work with interesting and dynamic people, be aware of where we are in our lives and work, and become valued, effective, whole people in valued and effective families and organisations. When we have to surrender and die to things, we want to be able to let go as easily as we can, suffer the least uncertainty and use the change creatively, to realise an even better situation than we left behind.

Organisations aspire to provide useful products and services, deliver increasing value for their share owners, manage efficient operations, enjoy competitive advantage and respect from their competitors, be timely innovators, offer a good and rewarding place to work, be humane and skilful in the endings, renewal and motivation of their people, and be good citizens wherever they are in the world.

We all want to play the game as engaged and empowered people. We don't want to waste unnecessary time, angst or resources. We want to show up well in the world and do good work. And we want to play with the big boys and hold our own.

How can we bring more of this about? What do we need to know and how can we discover it, sooner rather than later? What do we need to do and how do we best do it, and when?

What must we learn and how do we go about that? What has to end, what has to be invented and how do we find the passion, the fire in the belly that will keep us going?

Every journey has a story which brings meaning to the flow of events. We might tell our story as an adventure, a mystery, a revelation, a transformation, a drama, a soap-opera, a discovery, a documentary, a love story, or a mythic-hero's journey. Underneath the framework which we give the story, there are essential dynamics, the core drivers in our journey, from which all our stories are drawn. It is from these domains of experience that we take the raw material which we fashion into our story. It is at the level of these domains where we can actually change our journeys.

My work is dedicated to gaining personal and organisational leadership at the level of the core domains, where we can have real power to bring about potent journeys for ourselves and our fellow travellers. We get to the core through our stories. If we labour and lead at the core with the courage to engage the new and unknown, the stories will be retold with a change for the better.

I've spent a career coaching others and their work groups right at their core. Over the years patterns of inquiry and procedure have emerged. I've attempted to make these accessible as maps of the territory and useful explorations for you to employ. What follows is an introduction to the maps and trails and some essential sightseeing. The Insight Cycle is a good entry point for the whole adventure. The Cycle reveals:

- Four related domains of experience, common to organisations, groups and individuals, the core, generative drivers of our journey
- The interaction of the four concepts which generates personal and organisational change, learning and transformation
- Linkages to experiential methods for understanding the interaction of the domains and enhancing the journey at every level of organisation.

Reading The Maps: Glyphs, Concepts and Key Words

Each symbol and key word on any of the maps represents a concept. Each concept lives in a physical space on the map I call a 'domain', spaces where thoughts, feelings and experiences can be organised on the map. Each domain has a glyph associated with it, a graphic symbol which conveys a meaning. Glyphs visually stimulate our minds with the essence of the concept held in the domain. I've also chosen a word in English to provide a broad identity for each domain.

There has always been contention within myself and with others about which key words are the perfect words to use. Increasingly, picking just the right words to describe the domain has become impossible.

With this writing I've made the assumption that a glyph is a more important signifier of the meaning of the domain than the keywords. Domains become useful when we apply them in specific contexts with appropriate language. Given the myriad languages and cultures within which the Cycle and its derivative methods must be useful, a universal glyph and its concept can have a thesaurus of words behind it, any of which may be the perfect handle for the work being done. It is important for you to understand the concept of the domain and pick the right word based on what you are trying to accomplish. If the concept is understood and honoured, you will find good local language, and the map will do its work.

Stories

We all have a story to tell. How we see the world and our place in it, and how we see ourselves challenged or stuck or succeeding will define the context and style of the story. Our job as coaches, leaders, managers, parents and people is to make a positive difference in how all of our stories work out. While it may be nice or nasty to hear the story, we need access to making a difference at the core, the place from where the story actually arises.

We don't want to be an audience, cheering or booing from the sidelines. We want the powers to get inside the story where the storyteller, be it an individual or an organisation, is enabled to re-invent his or her story in a desirable way. We make up all our descriptions of life and work, stories of our becoming, using a combination of four underlying elements, described below. Now to draw the cycle and then to understand the concepts, language and relationships of the four domains.

The Cycle is a simple drawing, in the effortless style of cave drawings and hieroglyphics. We begin with a simple circle which implies a path. I started drawing the path at the three o'clock position, or, as I prefer, the East. So far it doesn't tell us much except that whatever it is, it repeats. Over and over, the path brings us back to wherever we started. To gain the powers of the cycle we need to add some stops along the route.

Situation

Our first core domain is 'Situation'. The glyph is a simple box shape. Our situation is the collection of physical conditions, outcomes, results, performance measures, money in the bank, cars in the garage and so on, which we use to define how things stand for us in the world. Organisations might describe their situation with performance measures, numbers of products, size of the customer base, total investment portfolio, number of offices, market share and such. I might describe my situation by the number of credit cards I have, or my physical age, the number of grey hairs left, age of my children, the count of dinners with good friends, or number of rooms in my home.

Every measure, outcome, result, or condition in 'Situation' is treated as completely neutral. For example, if I have a €20 note in my pocket, it is just a €20 note. It isn't good, it isn't bad. It isn't a lot. It isn't a little. It is just the fact of twenty Euros. A company produces 11,364 widgets in the month of May. That score goes in 'Situation'. It is not good performance or bad performance in 'Situation'. It is just the score, just a number. This neutrality is essential to the workings of the Cycle. It is required to conduct useful inquiries and reveal potent access to making positive differences in our journey.

Behaviour

 For our next domain, we follow the path of the Cycle onward, travelling halfway around to the West. The glyph is a stylised arrowhead. It implies motion and action and represents the concept of what we do. Our 'Behaviour' for short.

Individually, 'Behaviour' is our doings and not doings, our actions, steps and moves. At the organisational level 'Behaviour' is our business processes, procedures and systems, in action. Not the system design, but how the system or procedure or team actually, measurably behaves. Behaviours are the physical, demonstrable expressions we make in the world. For example, we get in the car and drive to work. The order entry process loses three orders a month. Telephone sales people deliver the same friendly response whether the order is for a pair of €10 socks or a €500 coat.

The 'Doing' Axis

If 'Situation' and 'Behaviour' were the only domains, we would have a very simple process to describe our journey around the Cycle. We find ourselves in a situation and we respond with behaviour designed to improve our conditions. Now, we can put an East-West 'Doing' axis on our cave drawing.

When we are operating exclusively on the 'Doing' axis, we behave, we get a result, we behave more to improve on a good result or recover a bad result, and a changed set of results may or may not ensue. And on and on.

I had a witty colleague years ago who said that her company was full of 'human doings.' I think she was talking about an organisation with a huge bias to being busy and putting points on the scoreboard, driven to hurry up and deliver results without a lot of so-called 'navel gazing,' which another colourful human doing I know likes to call the process of thinking.

For example, as a baby, the situation we perceive is pretty limited. Empty or full. Wet or dry. Alone or together. The behaviour available to improve our conditions is equally limited. It is mostly noise. We can cry or coo. Mothers learn to read the subtleties quickly and know when food or a diaper change are required. We cry, we are fed. We cry, we get changed. We cry, nothing happens. We cry louder. People come running. Simple, extremely effective once upon a time. Most of us still use the same scheme!

Organisations define and manage themselves in the domains of 'Behaviour' and 'Situation'. Just read any shareholder document. They invested and reorganised and hired and fired and acquired – all 'Behaviour'. They are worth this much now, have this profit margin, and own some percentage of this or that market – all 'Situation'. Most of us, for most of our lives, go on living on the 'Doing' line, expecting that our choices of action will largely fit the situation and produce decent results in our lives. It was a pretty good approximation for the best part of the 20th century. It's not such a good bet anymore.

Influence

Our behaviour is converted to a revised physical situation by the time we arrive at the East. How does this occur? We need a new domain, which I will draw halfway along the Cycle in the North. Whatever is in this domain, it is a transformer which takes our behaviour and acts on it in some way to convert it into a changed situation in the East.

For example, the baby cries and that noise becomes a full stomach. How does that happen? Mum, is the easy answer. Mother is the ultimate force in the baby's life. The baby does not realise that. But, we know, from our perspective that it is true.

Lao Tzu writes in the Tao Te Ching:
Tao produced the One.
The One produced the two.
The two produced the three.
And the three produced the ten thousand things.

The glyph at the true north of the Cycle is a set of three arrows all impacting one another at a point of focus. These three produce the vast complexity of stuff in the world. The key word I've chosen for this concept is 'Influence'. People and things and systems have the power to exert influence on ourselves and our organisations. Influence is a complex system of physical creation which runs constantly and which is way beyond anyone's comprehension, much less control. For example, the weather system produces rain and ice and sunny days. The force of technology, driven by the work of millions of people, moves us from wood fire to oil fire to hydrogen fire for our vehicles. As this occurs, it brings huge changes in organisational and individual situation.

The Behaviour in the West of the Cycle always occurs within this vast system of influence, placed here in the path. We behave and it immediately moves us to the North, where our behaviour shows up in interaction with the influences which surround us.

Influences are anyone and anything that takes our time up and asks something of us, whether to believe in them, serve them, feed them, answer their questions, pray to them, bow before them or make them feel important. Influences are also the systems, people or things which supply us with needed resources, whether spiritual, intellectual, emotional or physical. And, influences are the physical laws that govern the fundamental operation of all things. Throw the ball up, it comes down. Gravity is an absolute influence, a force of nature over which we have no say.

We may believe or assume that we have a say with some influences. I suggest that this is an illusion, brought about by their cooperation with us, rather than any direct control. I can't make you feel bad. Only you can do that. But I can intend to do that and say some pretty nasty stuff. If you choose then to feel bad, that is really you cooperating with my intent. Sad, but true. So, the Cycle works with influences as a one-way street – from them to us. The influences that count are always bigger than we are.

My most important influences are my wife and children, gurus of various sorts, a few very dear friends, the value of my social security payments, Apple's product introduction schedule, the cat, and a few compatriots who are gatekeepers to interesting work to be done.

Influences on an organisation could be trends in customer preference, supplier relationships, tax laws, trends in technology, government laws and regulations, cultural orientations, falling confidence in corporate honesty and morality, and the cost of rental space in downtown London.

In a team, we see our immediate clients and suppliers as primary influences, along with the organisational pay scheme and the organisational strategy to which we must deliver. As in the domains of 'Behaviour' and 'Situation', 'Influence' is neutral.

Mind

We have one last point on the compass to visit to complete the domains of the Cycle. Let's return to what I called the 'Doing' line. I act, the world of influences takes that and a new situation is established.

What must the domain at the South point of the Cycle hold, to convert the situation into a choice of behaviour? Another transformer, the reverse of influences, which processes situations into actions.

This is the human ability to perceive conditions, interpret them into good or ill, and invent and decide on actions which are designed to best enhance or recover the situation, given the influences. I've called this domain the 'Mind'. The glyph for 'Mind' is a bowl. Once again this idea springs from the ancient traditions of human observation where our consciousness is characterised as a container. A bowl is an ancient symbol, one that might appear on the cave wall to represent the domain of 'Mind'.

The domain of 'Mind' holds my beliefs, assumptions, mental models, experience, dreams and aspirations, intentions, passions and urges. Also my biases and prejudices and psychological patterning, the results of my inculturation at the hands of my parents and community and schools and bosses and religious scheme. My joy, my love, and my rage. All the filters through which I perceive the world.

For an organisation, the domain of 'Mind' holds strategy, mission, brand, policies, rules and regulations, both spoken and unspoken. The so-called glass ceiling, above which some classes of people may not be promoted, is a product of the unspoken, organisational 'Mind'. We have arrived at the domain where values are naturally placed on situation, influence and behaviour. Up to now I have been very careful to avoid any judgement in these domains.

Remember the €20 note I found in my pocket in the 'Situation' example? It was simply a €20 note. Not a good one or a bad one. No value judgements allowed. So it is in the domain of 'Behaviour'. I wave my hand at a passing taxi while I hold the €20 note. That is just an action. A behaviour. On its own, it means nothing. It has no value within the domain of 'Behaviour'. Likewise with the domain of 'Influence'. The influence called weather is neither good nor bad. The probability of a hurricane every year is a big influence on us if we live in the Caribbean islands. In and of itself, it is neither good nor bad, just a probability. Likewise a boss who never says good morning to me, is just a person who doesn't do good mornings. Not bad or good in the domain of 'Influence'. But, dammit, I sure experience the guy as a sour pickle before 10am. Which brings us to the seat of that 'dammit', the domain of 'Mind'.

In my 'Mind', if I make €500 a day, I will likely value the €20 note in my pocket as spare change. The price of a light lunch. If I make €5 an hour, I value the €20 as half a day's salary. The other guy's light lunch looks like a once-a-month, special night out to me. If I am a weather researcher, I may value the potential of a Caribbean hurricane as a swell adventure and opportunity. If I own a couple of beach hotels, I value it as a serious threat to my situation.

Everything depends on what is contained in my, or our collective, bowl of 'Mind'. Our mind holds models of how the world is, our place in it and how to behave to keep our situation stable and continually improved. Our mind is also capable of imagining completely new situations and generating the passion which fuels us to act mightily in the world of influence to realise our intentions.

It appears that humans possess three minds.
- An emotional mind which speaks in physical sensations and moods we refer to as our 'Heart'.
- A thinking mind which forms concepts and pictures and uses logic and language. We refer to this mind as the 'Head'.
- A kinaesthetic, physical mind – the seat of our body memory, our urges to get into motion and action, from where we ultimately act out our physical existence – the mind of our 'Hands and Feet'.

There is no guarantee that at any one moment these three minds are aligned with each other. When we have completely changed our mind, it will be accomplished in all three. Easier said than done. A dear friend of mine holds that changing one's mind is easy. Happens in a snap of the finger. Bing. "There, I've changed my mind." I think such finger-snap mind changes are typically handled with our head and only when there is no emotional attachment to the outcome.

Our emotions have deep memories and take lots of time and real experience to accomplish a true change of heart. When a business partner swipes all the money and heads for Mexico, how long will it take for the person left in Chicago with the empty bank account to conjure up anything like a warm feeling for that partnership, or any other, ever again?

And likewise our bodies. Our hands and feet learn through plenty of repetitions. Once learned, the reps are very hard to forget. Could you unlearn how to ride a bicycle? Anyone tried to unlearn a bad habit in a golf swing lately?

If I have grown up with a deeply held belief which is the foundation of a forty-year world view, and that belief is thrown into question by a world which no longer works as that belief demands, changing my mind to accommodate the new world may well be the hardest journey I will ever take.

The organisation which believed in video tape rental as their destiny never made the change.

Any one of the three minds can lead, but all three must get through the transition before we can really say we have actually 'Changed our Minds.'

The 'Being' Axis

We can now draw a second axis on the Cycle, connecting 'Mind' with 'Influence'. I call this the 'Being' axis. Between them, the two poles of the 'Being' axis hold all the complexity and mysteries of the world beyond ourselves and the world within. Engaging this axis calls on our curiosity, patience, humility, and a willingness to endure uncertainty and ambiguity. On this axis be dragons. The unknown. Whether we are individuals wanting more of life, or an industry needing to re-invent itself, we must spend time on the 'Being' axis, acquiring insight and new perspectives just as we let go of the old.

On the 'Being' axis we find the primary drivers of change. The domain of 'Influence' is always stirring and shifting. If our principal influences are among those in flux, we will be forced to change our minds to adapt, cope or become new people in a new game. The domain of 'Mind' is also endlessly stirring. Whether individually, as we age and stage through life, or organisationally as we have new ideas and aspirations and insights and strategies. If either end of the axis moves, the other must play catch up.

If we walk over and stand on the 'Doing' axis, the domains of 'Influence' and 'Mind' appear as necessary transformers for choosing behaviour and getting results. If we return and stand on the 'Being' axis, the domains of 'Behaviour' and 'Situation' appear to supply us with useful experience which reveals what we really believe and how the world really works. Engaging both 'Doing' and 'Being' in equal measure gets plenty done while we constantly learn, change and renew ourselves and our organisations.

Riding the Cycle

Transition, change, learning, renewal, rebirth, invention started with somebody's change of mind. It may have been stimulated by an earthquake, an unalterable force of nature, but the resulting adaptation and becoming of the humans involved, occurred in the mind. What makes our story interesting is the progress and evolution and transformation of mind as it dances with the world.

The interactive journeys of the four domains produce continual tensions in the Cycle. The possibility that the Cycle can ever be truly stress-free is not worth talking about. Every domain is turbulent, unpredictable, surprising.

The most practiced behaviour of a championship athlete or performer may appear to the untrained eye to be mechanically precise. But to the experienced coach or the performer themself, their action is full of nuance and difference, experiment and discovery. This most well-rehearsed display of talent represents the Cycle for the performer. Learning is required. Some change of mind, some difference in situation, a new request or alignment for a key influence. No matter how perfected the behaviour, it will still occur with a degree of uncertainty and error or possibility and surprise, depending on how we interpret it.

Situation is a factual measure of physical conditions. But there are vast uncertainties and room for error in how we actually measure them. Influence is the ten thousand things. Really a zillion things. When we attempt to contemplate the immensity, our brains hurt.

One science of mind suggests there are more than one hundred and fifty sub-personalities at work within us. Each with a point of view. Each with experience. Each with a head, heart and feet component. And all competing for attention and a voice. Our dynamic ecology of mind is as diverse and surprising as is the dynamic ecology of influence.

Increasingly the world seems to be going faster and faster. Influences are changing more frequently, driving more rapid changes in our behaviour in the face of the new situation. Technology, knowledge formation, shorter product cycles, the increase in advertising and marketing, the hyper speed of messaging and email versus physical mail services and all the rest serve to increase the frequency and extent of new tensions in the Cycle. As this happens, the world seems to run away from the state of our being, forcing more and more change of mind.

Some of the stories we tell ourselves imply that we can make transitions from one stable state to another. But when we really look at the dynamics of the Cycle, it is clear that the game never stops. It keeps going. The Cycle cycles. Endlessly. There is no such thing as a changeless time. We may have periods of less or more uncertainty driven by more or less tension between domains. No matter how small our change of mind, an effect on the ten thousand things will register. Other minds will have to change.

What makes transformation of mind the slowpoke in the Cycle is that our minds are carried around in human bodies. If changing our mind did not involve our head, heart and feet, it would be easier and faster. If changing our mind did not run headlong into the other drive to maintain a healthy status quo, which comes from our immune system, it would be easier and faster yet.

Our work is to become masters of the art of changing our minds.

Working The Cycle

When we are confronted with a story which needs help, we use the Cycle to understand and elaborate the story in the four domains where we can get some access to changing minds.

Finding the Four Domains in the Story

Our first job is to make sure we have story material for every domain on the board. What sells novels and movie scripts are dynamic situations, conflicting influences, changing, twisted, inspired and struggling minds, and the surprising behaviour which springs from the inevitable collisions. But people often leave out up to three of the four domains in their story.

A financial analyst does just that by describing company 'Situation' measured solely in profit and loss. The Personnel department reports on employee attitudes and mood – measures of 'Mind'. The Marketing team tracks changes in the 'Influence' called 'consumer expectations'. Production managers offer a history of the operation of the order entry process, a story of pure 'Behaviour'. None of these domains, taken by itself, is very interesting.

Here's a simple story: My daughter has three really close friends at home in America. She lives in Europe now. She believes that she will lose them if she is not in constant contact. She assumes that they are missing her as much as she is missing them. She sends long, daily emails and makes many phone calls to them. For every ten emails she sends, she receives one in return. A short one at that. She is increasingly fearful, even convinced that she is losing those friendships.

How do we go about working with the Cycle to change my daughter's story for the better?

It appears that all the domains are represented. 'Situation' is living in Europe. 'Mind' is the feelings and assumptions of losing her friends. 'Behaviour' is hyper-emailing. We don't know some things about what the 'Influences' are doing, but we do know who they are and we have some history about their ways from past experience.

Sanity Check the Logical Flow

Putting the story elements into the domains must reveal a clockwise logic in the story. If it isn't there, then we have to dig into the content of the domains and the links between them to locate the logical breakdown, which may well be the reason for the unhappy story in the first place.

For my daughter's story, even without all the details of the real operation of the influences, we can still see if what we do know fits the circular relationships in the Cycle.

My daughter's situation puts her away from her home where she has a few good friends.

In her head, she imagines a worst fear about what may happen. Her heart is heavy in missing her pals, and she feels they must be just as lonely. Her feet urge her to run away, back to America. However, she assumes that she is stuck in Europe with the immovable objects (the big influences) called Mum and Dad.

Her behaviour consists of a blizzard of emails and phone calls across the Atlantic.

So far so good. It hangs together. A lonely kid, stuck away from home, writes constant letters to fill the void and avoid losing her relationships.

We don't know much about the influences yet, except that, at the going away party they held, they all pledged their undying love, that they were missing her already and of course they would write as often as possible.

A new situation has occurred. Her letter sending has been transformed, through the Influences, into a few, short emails in return. One for every ten she sent.

Does the cycle hang together? Yes, given that we don't know how the ten thousand things turned fifty outbound emails into five, inbound. By organising the story around the domains and telling it with a logical flow, the story has now revealed itself to be a logical, mystery story, centred on the nature of the Influences. "How come they aren't writing back to me?" is the question of the hour.

Use the Known to Infer the Unknown

When we are missing data, or the story gets stuck, we have to speculate, using what we do know about the domains to infer information for empty or illogical domains. Speculation brings some uncertainty and we will have to assume a range of possibilities for the story. This is better than nothing.

If our first level speculation does not get anywhere, we have specific and profound procedures to apply, linked to specific domains. Any of the procedures can be used on their own, or in any context of the Cycle.

For my daughter's story, we can work directly in the framework of the Cycle, without using bigger tools. The domain in question is 'Influence'. A speculation about what may be going on with her friends is straightforward. She sends ten long emails as an input. She gets one short one back as an output. So,

"What must be the actual story of the Influences domain?"
The answer to this is a brainstorm. A make-it-up exercise. We need to get lots of ideas and find some patterns before we are confident to go forward. Ten minutes after asking this question, we had the first emerging pattern of ideas:

"The girls back home do not have the time to write many or lengthy emails and they are doing the best they can."

With this we had a completely workable story around the Cycle. There was one, tiny mind change already: the story had ceased to be about 'Do they miss me?' It had become a question of:

"How to get the most meaning from the short time they might have?"

Add up the Transformational Drivers

When the imbalance in the Cycle is in the extreme, we can assume that the humans involved must accomplish changes of mind which will take up some or much of their energy and attention for some while. How to determine when a change is sufficiently turbulent to generate resistance and waste?

We can examine each domain for the size and frequency of endings, reinventions and commitments which must be accomplished. The more we find, the more imbalance and resulting uncertainty in the Cycle. The more imbalance and uncertainty, the larger the collective change of mind.

The concept of Ending, Reinvention and Commitment comes from the TransforMAP, which is the map of the journey humans take to complete a change of mind.

Endings

We can take each domain of the Cycle and examine the potential for endings to occur.

Endings are afoot when influences change their impact. This could be the loss of a loved one or the sudden irrelevance of a specific technology on which our business has depended or the arrival of a monsoon.

Situation endings occur when we move to another town. Winning the lottery ends our excuse for working. We used to have a private office and now we share a hot desk with everyone else.

Behaviour endings are pretty obvious. When work started to arrive digitally via a computer screen and not in heavy brown envelopes hand-delivered to the desk, we certainly saw that as an end to familiar office behaviour.

Endings of mind occur when a way to think about something is no longer operational. For example, the end of the Santa Claus belief for kids. The end of viewing myself as immortal. Corporate strategies must end when they no longer work. Products are no longer built and organisational identity and brand die away.

Reinvention

Experiments bring the unknown with them. They bring uncertainty as we set aside what we think we know, to explore what may be possible. Entering the possible brings the likelihood of change and change of mind. Perhaps we have to go looking for new influences and run a communications experiment with twenty-five of our best customers. Individually we allow no coffee in our situation for a couple of months to see if we feel better. An experiment in organisational mind finds us setting aside our present strategy and figuring out different marketing strategies for three different markets. For organisational behaviour, we convert our second production line to a team-based approach to see if it makes any positive difference.

Commitment

Transformational stories always include the rise of burning intentions, making passionate decisions and commitments, and the work to make something new come true. Whenever these realisation processes occur, a great many mind changes will be required.

For example, we decide, in mind, that making the best chocolate ice cream in the world is our consuming mission. In the 'Behaviour' domain we build the processes and install the skill base to make the best product. We also put a rigorous cost control system in place. We choose the consumer trend of seeking higher and higher quality of food as the principal influence which we will follow for our brand and product mix. We also pick twenty worldclass grocery organisations as our only influence for distribution. In the 'Situation' domain, we have six flavours, three package sizes and are turning €3.4 million annually.

More Horsepower

When the organisation of the story into domains and logical checks and simple speculation are not enough, it is time to engage the procedures derived from the Cycle. There are four and each has a fundamental link to one of the domains in the Cycle. Each procedure is described in detail in its own chapter.

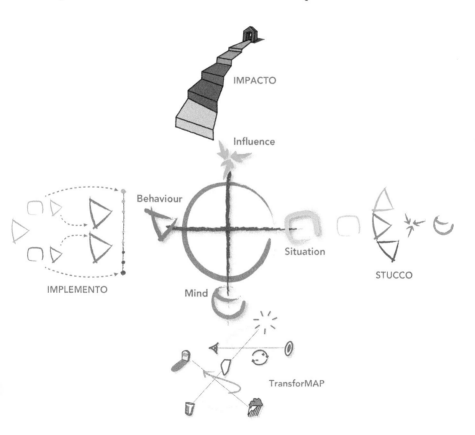

Situation and Stucco

I link our 'Stucco' procedure directly to the domain of 'Situation'. Often, we cannot seem to improve the results we are getting, no matter what we attempt: from changing the size of our waistline to figuring out why the paychecks never come out on time or our software has too many errors in it. When our situation is stalled in a negative condition we are likely caught in a degenerative loop of actions and results, mired in a grand mess. Stucco is an inquiry and inference procedure which uses the domains of the Cycle in a specific way to find the root cause of the loop and find optimal experiments to run which reveal the way out of the mess.

Behaviour and Implemento

When our behaviour stalls, or when it is not producing desirable results, we are usually caught in a dilemma, big uncertainty, or are pretty out of touch with how the world works. We don't have enough information to make a decision and then to act.

When I am unsure about the next, right thing to do, I employ our Implemento procedure. Implemento is based on the logic of the Cycle and will reveal what we truly want and need to accomplish and a success path which we can use as a temporary structure to keep moving. I use Implemento for:

- dilemma wrangling
- when I don't know where to start
- optimising my current practices which need adaptation to a new situation
- when I am not sure what I want my situation to become
- understanding how my critical influences actually work.

Influence and Impacto

I link Impacto with the 'Influence' domain. Impacto is a superior method for enrolling our most important influences into our journeys. Impacto weaves all the domains of the Cycle into a logical story. It provides a balanced process for telling and listening. In a conscious, honest organisation, such a comprehensive framework is required for group communications from leaders down as well as from the bottom up.

Mind and the TransforMAP

The principal link to a method from the domain of 'Mind' is the TransforMAP. Organisations making big changes cause lots of people to have to change their minds through many endings, reinventions and commitments. Forcing a change of mind on to people produces resistance, uncertainty and waste. The TransforMAP is a map of the journey we each take to change our mind, whether learning, transforming or renewing ourselves. It is also a scheme for listening, reflecting and supporting which acknowledges the complexity of the transformation at hand and which keeps us moving on the journey.

A Brief Summary

We can interpret the life and interaction of the domains of the Cycle as a story of change, learning, development, renewal, or even simply as a story of living. Life is birthing, learning, renewing, changing, performing, achieving, arriving, leaving, growing and dying.

Life is a dance between doing and being. The dance can be viewed as the play of the four domains through time. Why bother finding the four threads in our story? Because we want to have the best dance we can. Simple as that. Why have less of a dance than is available to us with a bit of work to release us from the past and open the possibility of the future?

With the powers provided through the logic of the Cycle we give individuals and organisations access to their complete story at the essential level where the story can be transformed with an explicit, rational change of mind. We predict the dimension of transition effects on people, enable and coach complete transformations, break performance log jams, invent ways forward in high uncertainty and bring the others along with us as quickly as possible.

We can predict the dimension of uncertainty we will cause in a coming change by estimating how many endings, reinventions and passionate commitments to a new world we will need to achieve within the business-as-usual schedule.

Rising uncertainty puts behaviour on hold. Using Stucco, Implemento, Impacto and the TransforMAP opens the door to possibility and exploration – an appropriate strategy for uncertain times.

When we get stuck in a mess and our situation just will not get better, no matter what we do, the Stucco procedure can be used to break the degenerative cycle.

When uncertainty is too high to decide how to move ahead, Implemento will reveal a success path which we can use as a temporary structure to keep moving.

Impacto is a superior method for enrolling our most important influences into our journeys. Impacto weaves all the domains of the Cycle into a logical story. It provides a balanced process for telling the story of our behaviour and listening, a comprehensive structure for communications.

I think of the Insight Cycle as a framework as much as a tool. I actually see TransforMAP in the same light. These are useful in the enigmatic and transcendent zones of the work. They are like real maps, for sensemaking, finding a way in unknown territory. I see Stucco and Implemento more as procedural tools, designed for right now problem-solving. Impacto falls somewhere in the middle, with heavy leanings toward the tool category.

The following chapters introduce each of the maps in turn, outlining their core function and usefulness, describing the different domains named on the map, how the maps can be used in practice and offering some practical guidance in each case for managing a real conversation.

Stucco

We turn to Stucco when the Insight Cycle has become imbalanced or stuck, and none of our previous attempts to get 'unstuck' seem to have made any difference. Stucco uses the 'Situation' domain of the Insight Cycle as its starting point and allows us to explore fresh perspectives.

Stucco is a procedure for discovering the root causes of an undesirable downward spiral in our current cycle of behaviour, influence, situation and mind – what we call a 'mess'. When we feel as if, whatever we try, we're taking two steps forward and three steps back.

We may think that we are the victims of a cruel circumstance or we may realise we are the architects of our own struggle. Either way, the mess continues to exist because no matter how we have attempted to change behaviours, play the influences or redefine and reorganise the situation, we still lack a key insight into a predictable way of breaking the patterns of behaviour, influence, situation and mind from which the mess arose.

Stucco gets beyond hunches, guesswork and limited, linear 'fix-it' thinking. It was crafted to deliver genuine changes in the architecture of our ways.

Stucco reveals the structure and the roots of the dynamics in play through a process of data gathering, mapping, integrative pattern making, and linear analysis of the relationships between the patterns before redesign and creating a new cycle.

If you are a Star Trek fan, or have been intrigued by films

like 'Back to the Future', the 'Terminator' series, or 'The Tenth Monkey', you already know about the space-time continuum. You know that time travellers can, and likely already do, return from the future and make adjustments in the present to change the time line, creating an alternative future in the attempt to avoid some future catastrophe. Applying Stucco reminds me of time travel.

We begin with a messy situation that seems to constrain us. We work backward in time and space to discover the root cause which has propagated through time in countless ways. To do this we:

- define our situation as a set of measurable conditions
- exhaustively catalogue behaviour which seems to produce the conditions we are experiencing
- infer a set of influences which are necessary and sufficient to convert our behaviours into these conditions.

With this comprehensive view of behaviour, influence and situation we turn to the likely core of the mess: the beliefs, assumptions, strategies and mental models held in our minds. Standing back from the scene to gain a consulting perspective, we adopt a 'witness' point of view. As witnesses rather than participants, we define the roots of the mess by:

- inferring the set of beliefs, assumptions and mental models which must be operational if we act as we do in the face of our critical influences and real conditions.

From this insight into operating beliefs we are free to postulate a practical transition which can break the cycle: a definable, measurable change of mind. We can invent and embark on a defined and rational learning path to a new situation which is much more to our liking. Now, we can truly change the time line. We begin by:

- inventing positive alternatives for any questionable belief
- postulating appropriate behaviours from the perspective of this new belief
- playing the trial behaviours through the critical influences to see if our situation improves.

We continue this logical exploration until we land on a set of trial mental models and alternative behaviours which we believe will better serve us. We combine these into experiments which we can enthusiastically engage in the real world and get to work.

What follows is a definition of the language of Stucco and a description of the Stucco procedure, step by step.

Articulating the Mess

Situation	Doings	Forces	Beliefs

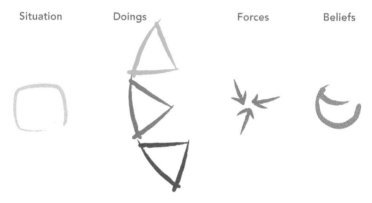

Start by describing what seems to be stuck, as both a story and a set of specific measures, in enough detail that we can relate specific things we do, or don't do, to the landscape as we are experiencing it. We need the overview story so we can perceive every aspect of our lives or businesses that is involved.

Situation

Most of the time, most of us describe a mix of overall and specific conditions as the basis for our actions. This is simple cause and effect thinking. An outcome I experience 'makes' me react in some way. And I get another outcome as a result of my re-action. And so on. This is not the case, but it is handy shorthand, most of the time.

In Stucco, the definable, measurable elements which make up what the Insight Cycle refers to as our 'Situation' are the starting point of what we are trying to change or break free from. We define it in family, social, political, business, economic, physical and psycho-emotional terms to mention a few. This web of personal circumstance is the ground from which we select what needs doing and not doing, the background of our day-to-day experience. Elements of this web rise up on a daily basis to demand our attention and drive our agenda of action and reaction.

Doings

In some measure, the situation also results from our previous decisions, actions and inaction. These are the next areas to examine.

By all generally accepted standards, there are the right things we should be doing to run our business effectively. MBA schools teach accepted practices. Gurus write books about how to do it right. However we got the idea, there are actions, steps, completions, expenditures, investments, acquisitions, divestments, hirings, firings, and so on that we believe are correct, appropriate and ought to be effective. But, to borrow a song title, it ain't necessarily so.

These we call 'Right Doings'. Not morally right, but generally correct based on popular practice. Begin with right doings. Make a list of the actions we take which we assume are the best we can do. List as many as you can think of. Don't worry if they seem a bit tangential or unrelated. More is better. While you are at it, make notes in the 'Situation' domain about what the conditions are which tell you that the actions you are taking are the right ones.

Then there are 'Wrong Doings'. Make another list with these. Wrong doings are in the class of 'damned if we do and damned if we don't'. Wrong doings are not morally wrong. They are actions which we would prefer to avoid because we know that they will probably contribute to our mess. Yet we feel compelled to do them because of other circumstances. Perhaps we are pretty burned out and we need a round of golf a couple of times a week to just unwind. But doing that means we are not calling the meetings with clients that might make a positive difference in the business. Or the investment community is being ferocious about our quarterly earnings. Yet, effort to accommodate those demands defeats us in investing in what we must do to be healthy in the long run. Again, add to the list in the 'Situation' domain – this time we want the conditions which seem to be forcing you to make these sub-optimal actions you feel you must take.

Finally, we have 'Not Doings'. Most of us recognise possible actions which might well improve our circumstances, but we do not do them for some good reasons, or even bad reasons. These are things, not done, which could have been done, or could still be done, to make a difference. For example, suppose our life partner is also our business partner and relations are strained at home. We feel it's necessary to compensate by making zero demands at work, even though the mess we are in appears to sit squarely in their department.

Often we don't do things because they appear, or will actually be, too risky. Perhaps we've had the idea that we could really improve the company by shutting down for a month, rearranging the players and the furniture and installing a new digital infrastructure. But the challenges in doing that appear to hold too many uncertainties and we do not make a start. Add to the list with what it is you know is possible but you are not choosing to do. Add the 'why-we-didn't-do-that' to the list of conditions driving behaviour in the definition of situation.

Forces

Forces are the influences on our businesses and lives which we have little or no control over. Usually, these are big entities, powerful people, major trends and essential physical laws. Like gravity. The boss. Mum. Inland Revenue. The Computer. A Cure for Cancer. The Supreme Court. The Bank of England. The World Wide Web. A colleague of mine has identified about 120 of these strong influences which move at their own pace and in their own directions.

At the beginning of work with Stucco almost everyone identifies forces which they consider being outside their sphere of influence, but which are not forces at all.

For example, suppose I bake bread for a living. I believe deeply that my customers must have their product delivered on Monday before 9am. I perceive this to be a force: the will of the Customer. But the truth is that this so-called force is actually a policy which I created that is masquerading as something immutable. Maybe, long ago, I learned from my Dad that delivery on Monday before 9am was what God had intended. When I first called on clients I set that expectation in their minds by making that delivery day and time part of the offer. They may have had no particular need or expectation before I walked in. But I saw it as an unchangeable law of the bread making business and now my customers are used to it. In fact, they may experience me as a big force and believe that they can only get their bread from me on Mondays before nine. As I'm not getting any younger, it is harder and harder to meet this demand. However, this policy is within my personal influence to change. If I asked my customers when they actually need the product, the answer might be different.

Look over the action lists and the statement of the mess. It seems that no matter what you have tried and not tried, the mess remains. Therefore we could deduce that the world around us, i.e. the forces and important influences, must be operating in ways we do not fully understand. If we do not know, but we have some data about actions and results, we can make a world up. We can infer a reality in the world from our data.

For example, if our income is dropping yet we have more customers in the store than we ever had, we could infer that the force of the consumer culture has changed its purchasing habits. We could re-characterise the consumer force from 'big spenders' last year, when anyone who walked in bought something, to 'window shopping' this year when half the town is in the store every day and one out of a hundred make a purchase. Ask:

"What in the world must be going on here?"

We need this sketch for later when we begin testing new actions. And we need it to determine where something we think of as a force is really something of our own making and very much in our control.

Beliefs

When we are confronted with a set of conditions and we have a goal in mind, our natural reaction is to make a step. We decide what to do based on our internal belief structure, our mental model of how the world works. We believe or assume that the world works in certain ways. We construct a cause and effect logic based on these beliefs and then act based on that logic whether consciously or not.

For example, suppose I have had heartache and difficulty in a couple of close business partnerships. I have come to believe that I am not suited for such endeavours. Yet I dream of making films, which is a team effort if ever there was one. One day the dream opportunity shows up where I can be a filmmaker and partner with someone who I genuinely like and who is truly gifted. But, because of my mental model, I hesitate and find other ways to be busy on my own so that I will not screw up my life one more time with what will surely wind up as a failed partnership and a lost friend.

Very often we do not really know our beliefs, or we are unwilling to recognise them. Then we have some logical work to do. We have created three sets of data to use here: the patterns of situation, patterns of doings and the sketch of the forces. We are poised to look at our behaviour as accurately as we can, and to look at the conditions around us which prompted that behaviour, and then to figure out why we make the choices we do.

The 'why' is our mind. At the organisation level it may be a policy or a tradition or a component of our strategy. Personally it may be habit or belief, assumption, mental model, or even the genetic arrangement of our personality.

We can make educated guesses about what a person would have to believe to act as we did, given the circumstance. It helps to stand back, take a detached position and speculate on the beliefs that would make sense of the pattern of our actions – right doings, wrong doings, not doings – in response to the current situation. Ask:

"If visiting aliens were to observe us in action, what beliefs would they assume we must hold to be making these choices

**in the face of the forces in play and the situation we are trying
to influence?"**

By acting in this way, we are less likely to be defensive or try to
justify what we have done – they are just doings and we are simply
exploring the context that seems to underpin them. As witnesses,
rather than participants, we get to the root of the matter, by
inferring the set of beliefs, assumptions and mental models which
must exist to account for why we act as we do in the face of our
critical influences and the circumstances we are trying to change.

We rarely find fast answers. This part of the process often
circles the real answer for a while. Beating around the bush. This
is rarely a pretty sight. In any event, if we give the process time and
keep at it patiently, the root beliefs and assumptions inexorably
make their way to the surface.

Beliefs and assumptions are at the core of the mess we find
ourselves in. They just always are.

Redesign: Creating a New Cycle

New Beliefs	New Doings	Forces	Situation

We can now use our work to shift the prevailing pattern and create
a more virtuous upward spiral to replace the vicious downward
cycle that is sustaining the mess.

New Beliefs

Changing our minds would force us to make different choices
which might lead to an improved outcome. Changing our mind
has two components. First we have to find a better mental model
to promote. Then we have to take that idea into the real world and
test it out in the heat of real people and real situations.

Figuring out a new belief takes some brainstorming of alternatives to the list of beliefs and assumptions which we have built. We can start by simply taking the opposite belief of any one on our list which seems important to us. We ask:

"What is the opposite of our belief?"

For example, from our earlier story, if the bread baker is stuck with the belief that:

"There is no one in the state who can bake bread as well as I can"

Then we create an opposite assumption to test:

"There is someone in this state who can bake bread better than I can."

Now this may not be optimal, but it rapidly suggests new inquiries to be made which may be a world changer for the baker and family. Because, if this bread man actually believed that, we can all bet that he would know who that person was. But he does not – yet. Write the alternative assumptions into the 'Mind' domain on the map. Now we take our new assumption for some test drives via the Insight Cycle:

New Doings

Brainstorm alternative behaviours which people who believe such things as the new beliefs would do.

Forces

Take those behaviours forward and test how the forces would impact them – they may need to be modified as a result.

Situation

Project a range of possible changes to the measures we are concerned with and add them to the 'Situation' domain.

Ventures

These new behaviours predicated on new beliefs look great on paper. But how will they translate to the real world? The work with Stucco creates plenty of material for potential ventures. Our job is to take that work and integrate it into one or two trials and then go do them and see what happens. Nothing much more than that is assumed or necessary.

We need to invent a smallish learning experiment which we can complete, say in a week or so. An exploration which will give us new first-level knowledge about the working validity of our alternative belief and trial doings, without sinking the ship.

We aren't looking for lifelong commitments here. We are experimenting. Learning. Testing. We are interested in how the forces work as much as anything else. With enough testing, our minds will indeed change. One day. The alternative belief will, over time, become a core belief, surrounded by direct experience to validate its status.

Back to the bread man. Trying out his alternative belief about there actually being somebody in the state who could bake as well as him led to some phone calls to the best bakery in the big city to talk to some colleagues in the business about where the best bread was being baked. Which led to meeting a couple of superb and inspired bakers. Which led to uncovering where the best people were being trained. Which led to an internship deal where superb younger bakers came to work and learned with our client. Which led to the changed belief that indeed,

"There is a handful of bakers in this state who are every bit as good as me and an abundance of younger people who want to learn from me, want to work hard, and have many years ahead to surpass my skill."

All it took was making the first call from the perspective that at least one great baker existed within a day's drive. Just like that, one change in our assumptions and the resulting experiments can lead to the situation improving or even a complete resolution of the mess.

Implemento

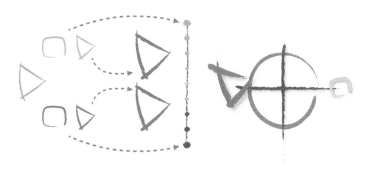

Implemento begins with the 'Behaviour' domain of the Insight Cycle, helping us to design wiser and more effective action.

What to do when there is nothing apparent to do? Where to head when everything seems temporary, uncertain, chaotic, un-clear? What to do when there is everything to do? A vast possibility for taking action. Where everything is a priority. What to do when impaled on the proverbial horns of a dilemma? Where either choice is equally the right choice? Where either choice is equally the wrong choice?

These conditions challenge us to find a new perspective on things. To rise above the apparent dilemma, to act on some deeper faith that things work out. To clarify our intentions and take action in the midst of uncertainty. They challenge us to act out of the reality of what confronts us, rather than acting out of past experience.

Implemento combines a rigorous situation analysis with an opportunity for innovation and 'making it up.' These two activities generally reveal a surprising perspective and clarity in the matter. The 'what we know' that we did not know we knew.

Implemento prompts us to create scenarios for the future based on an action which we believe would be best given the conditions at hand. The trick with Implemento is not to second guess what will happen. Take the plunge. Let our imagination run riot. Then take the time to reflect on the sum of our stories and build a comprehensive, multi-faceted, strategy for taking a first step.

Implemento offers the curious possibility of beginning with a molehill of direction and plans, giving that molehill to Implemento's structures and your imagination for an hour or so, and discovering a mountain of purposes, insights and steps to get on with the right stuff.

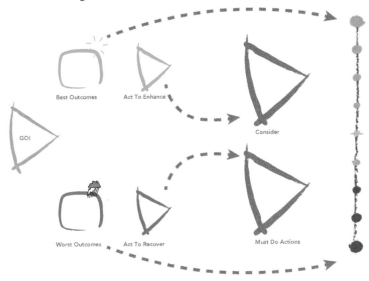

The Concept and Map

When we do stuff in the world we basically take actions, look at the results and take more actions. Any action can produce a range of results. In Implemento we define a worst and a best set of outcomes for every action: tangible, observable conditions which result directly from our doings. Best outcomes are the most desirable: a good mood, a book in print, money in the bank. Worst outcomes are a bad mood, losing a customer, jail.

If we get a best outcome we usually attempt to build on it, enhance it, make it even better. Therefore, each 'Best Outcomes' space is followed by an 'Act to Enhance' space, since a best-of-all-worlds result always frees you to make moves which make more of what you wish to do. If we get a worst outcome, our next action will surely be designed to reverse our fortunes and recover the situation. Therefore an 'Act to Recover' space always follows a 'Worst Outcomes' space, because, when lousy results begin, creative recovery steps can push outcomes in a more desirable direction.

The map eventually tells two stories or 'cases'. They share the same beginning: the action we first introduce. The endings differ, depending on which route each case follows through the map. Work begins on the left with a statement of an action we propose taking – the 'Go!' action. It proceeds to the right through possible results and more actions.

Over the Learning Edge

Using Implemento helps us free up our minds to 'make up' the answers, beyond the limits of what we might have previously thought about. Although 'making it up' may not sound very scientific, it actually is a matter of science. Just as our heart beats all our life, our minds are at work, day and night, seven days each week, responding to the events which we encounter and exploring possible options for our lives. In Western rationalist cultures, we commonly refer to this as our subconscious at work. Other cultures suggest we can also tap into other ways of knowing – premonition, intuition, prophecy and fate, for example. Many, including yours truly, believe we each can tap into a larger, collective unconscious experience.

Perhaps we do this when we sleep, perhaps all the time. If this is so, then our mind holds both our own personal perspective and an interactive access to a wider community perspective. Our status quo world view, which we know we know, is our everyday mental model. But in the shadows, our interaction with the larger system is stirring us up, threatening the status quo, and forming an emergent mental model, under our everyday surface.

Most of us are completely unaware of this formation process. It rarely raises its head above our usual noisy days. It seems to appear in dreams. And it also leaks out as a 'slip of the tongue,' or a surprise action which 'I just wouldn't normally do!'

Implemento requires that we find answers beyond the ordinary. Following the Implemento process out to the point where we have to start inventing the answers opens the door to the emergent material in our mind, which we don't yet know we know. Our mind finds the material it is chewing on, just under the surface and provides it to us as if we have just 'made it up.'

Our minds don't seem to work in random ways. There are patterns to our subconscious stirring. So, as we make up lots of answers, we see emergent patterns, across the board, no matter how far afield our inquiry reaches. Therefore, when we recognise a recurring idea over a few answers, we can be reasonably sure that our deeper mind is offering direction for us which we should consider. Implemento organises our answers and provides an elegant way to recognise and utilise these emerging patterns – the benefit of 'hindsight' before taking action.

Making the Cases

If the world were a linear, determinant, certain system of cause and effect we would have no use for Implemento. Fortunately, the world is a much more interesting, unpredictable, indeterminate, complex, semi-chaotic ocean of forces which our little boats of life and business sail on. No matter what we are up to, from going to the movies to going to the moon, there is always a measurable uncertainty which we can never know enough to entirely erase.

Using Implemento, we set out to determine the best step we can make now by brainstorming the possibility of all that might occur two or three steps further on. We do that by creating possible scenarios of action and results on the map. Developing the stories takes us into a world of exceptionally good and exceptionally bad results. These are not spaces most of us encounter every day and we don't really expect either one.

But working with these possibilities is essential to our growth and very useful.

We begin with the most desirable scenario, the 'Best' story. We make our 'Go!' action and the best happens and we act on that circumstance and things get even better. Only the most Pollyanna-ish or the biggest advocates of the-world-as-just-wonderful plan for this eventuality.

The second scenario is a seriously undesirable and finite possibility which describes the outer limits of Stinky. No one plans for this either, but they should, because 'Worst' stimulates some of the most creative thinking in the entire process.

When we invent each case, we do it as if it is really happening. Once we have claimed an action, we act as if that action has really been taken. Each outcome is now our reality, rather than a 'might be.' Wherever we are in a scenario, we are really there. Feeling it, smelling it, tasting it. We say "We are doing such and such", rather than "We would do so and so". We take enough time for our imagination to create a vivid experience of the results we are experiencing before choosing our next actions. We don't look back. Every case is its own story. Each outcome and act is a unique part of a unique story.

The next section describes the invention steps for each scenario in turn.

Go!

What are we going to do? Imagine doing it, completing it. Describe it in the 'Go!' domain. This is the action you are planning to take or thinking about taking. It is typically a statement describing the step or steps you have in mind. It should ideally contain a well-defined action or set of actions – an action that you or the group is considering in the near future; one that needs some thought put into it to ensure that it is the right action and that it goes well.

Implemento helps think through this action to explore the potential consequences and learn from them. If it's a dilemma, take one side and go with it. Then take the other side. If there are a million choices, take a couple. If there are no choices, make up something and run with it.

The action you pick does not have to be perfect, it will be adjusted and improved through the Implemento process.

Worst Outcomes

These are the worst possible outcomes that could result from the intended action. This should generate a list of outcomes that are stinky and not desired. It paints a gloomy picture of how bad the world could look if everything went wrong following the action being considered.

Include those things that concern you and seem as if they could happen, even if they are unlikely. Think about the impact of the action on yourself, on the people immediately around you and others involved, and on the wider system.

It is worth taking some time to move beyond the obvious answers in this process. On some occasions our first, fast answer is useful. That said, the really good stuff springs from a process of self-reflection, of listening more deeply to our emergent ideas. Use a question framed from one of the words below:

"What could be more ... awful, perverse, aggressive, dangerous, heavy?"

– and let the minds in the room toss it around without any time pressure, conversation, debate or criticism. It can be helpful to probe for more, to see if something new will emerge from behind the curtain of the obvious, somewhere beyond our habitual thinking. Then ask it a few more times without regard for getting an answer. Something worthy or crazy may appear and get to the map in either case. We can always toss it out later. Outcomes may include:

- The System – what quantitative factors have changed? What qualitative factors? What has increased? Decreased?
  - "Production quality has decreased by 30%"
  - "It takes twice as long to process the paperwork"
  - "There was a 50% increase in complaints about the elevators, so morale has gone down"

- Stakeholders – what are they talking about? Questioning? What are they doing? Acting on? What is their mood or attitude?
  - "The big bosses are in shock!"
  - "Customers are screaming!"
  - "Two customers dropped us but five more wanted us to give a discount."
- Ourselves – what are we feeling? Our mood and attitude? What are we thinking about? What do we need to do? Our thoughts, feelings and urges are as much a part of the outcomes as any physical change in things around us.
  - "I'm questioning my future. Was this the right choice or not?"
  - "I'm feeling guilty about the hurt we have caused"
  - "We're all headed out to bang on customers' doors".

Acts to Recover

As soon as things start to break down, we take recovery actions to get things back on track. Acts to recover push worst outcomes in more desirable directions before things get badly out of hand. This is the space for listing those actions that would need to be taken to recover if the worst outcomes occurred for real. Fast forward and imagine that you are in the world where the worst outcomes have happened. Stand in that future and imagine how it feels. Report the situation as if it were happening and ask what actions need to be taken now to get things back on track? What can be done to improve the situation?

If you get stuck for actions use the ideas below to suggest some new directions. There are four kinds of actions that others have found useful to ask about in considering moves to recover. There is nothing magic about them, feel free also to invent your own:

- *Communications:* for example, linking up with others to hear their opinions and ideas, inform or enrol them, get them on your side
- *Knowledge building:* for example, gathering information and data, alone or with others, doing research and design

- *Using Resources:* for example, investing more of your time, money, attention, energy and experience
- *Commitments:* for example, making decisions and choices.

Best Outcomes

These are the best possible outcomes that could result from the intended action. It is a list of the most positive outcomes from the steps described in the 'Go!' box. This is a picture of how things could look in the future. Imagine what this future would be like – how it would feel for us. For our team. For the world. As we complete entering our ideas in any domain on the map, we take a breather and find an additional question which seems to fit the direction we are exploring.

"What could be more ... colourful, joyful, complete, huge, satisfying, novel?"

Ask the question and let the minds in the room toss it around some more. Perhaps we know of someone who is very original in extreme times. If so, we can take them with us in our imagination, through any of the cases. We ask this alter ego the same questions again, adding 'their' ideas to our map.

Acts to Enhance

We've achieved more than we bargained for! After the champagne, what's the next step? We rarely allow ourselves to think beyond achieving the outcomes we want. 'Acts To Enhance' provides a space for thinking through what could be done to make things even better, or avoid the problems that can sometimes come with success, e.g. attention you don't want, orders you can't fulfil, complacency feeding subsequent decline, overwhelming demands on your time.

We may not be ready for these actions yet – we have to achieve the success first – but Implemento takes us to a place where we can explore them. Stand in the future, with your best outcomes as a firm foundation beneath your feet and take the time to imagine what might now be possible.

Imagine that the best outcomes have become reality. Live in that space for a while and tell that story. What actions could now be taken to turn those Best Outcomes into even better outcomes?

Many people respond to bad results with resentment, anger or acting out. Some avoid, pull back and go inside themselves to deal with their most personal, worst fears. So, too, success can also bring bad habits – people respond to it with relaxation, lost focus, big celebrations, or assuming they know something when they were just lucky or in the right place at the right time.

Our list of actions in every action space should be checked for personal, habitual, emotion-driven reactions which come from our personal history, but which may not best serve the real job of enhancement (or recovery). Very often our habits are completely counter-productive. The energy can be released in other ways and healthy futures will be served by thinking about what will really work best and contrasting that with our habitual knee-jerks.

Emergent Objectives and Actions

With our cases completed, we have the material we need to mine our lists of best outcomes, worst outcomes, enhancement actions and recovery actions. Our goal is a set of objectives and actions which optimize the 'how' and 'why' of what we want to achieve.

We begin with the 'why' we are going to take action. We will state each objective in the form of a measure to give us both directional information and to evaluate how far we have come in the direction we seek. With a set of measures established we can go to the action material and synthesize a set of actions which are likely to improve where we stand on each of our measures.

Measures – Ideal, Minimum Acceptable, Failure

Measures turn best and worst outcomes into something we can work with now, highlighting the most important factors to pay attention to. Measures help communicate a more complete description of what we want to achieve and give a sense of progress towards goals.

Braving Uncertainty

The best outcomes represent aspirations. These might include tangible and intangible measures, such as happiness, efficiency, relationships and communication. These overlap and interact to define what we want to achieve.

The worst outcomes help define the minimum. Left as worst outcomes they can discourage us from getting into action in the first place. Replacing worst outcomes with acceptable minimums enables a set of measures we can live with, defining the minimum results that the starting action has to deliver. We can transform our worst fears into a commitment to a fundamental standard of achievement.

Before diving into the data we need a framework for stating a meaningful, measure-based objective. Here is a simple scale with a top, a bottom and a middle. To know where we are we need to establish three numbers: the ideal, the minimum acceptable, and failure.

Ideal

Minimum Acceptable

Failure

Suppose we are measuring profits. We place the ideal amount – for example 20% – at the top of the scale. Meanwhile, we have to have at least 5% to keep our investors with us, so we call that the passing grade for us, calling that our minimum acceptable position. We know that we will go out of business if our profit goes below -2% for more than six months. So, that number is placed at the bottom. Now we have a measured objective described as a range of what we want and don't want, bottom line acceptable conditions and possibly where things stand today.

Read over the best and worst outcomes and attempt to find distinctive patterns in each. There will usually be some overlap between the patterns of best and worst outcomes which will suggest what measures are most significant for the action considered. The best outcomes will give some clues about measures of success. The worst will suggest measures of failure. For each scale we choose, also determine the minimum acceptable level. If we fall below this we will fail, but falling only to this level means we are still in the game with scope to recover. This will help in our communications with others – "we will not do worse than this" – and also determine for ourselves when it is time either to adjust or to declare the initiative a failure and start again with a fresh approach.

Revised Actions

We now have a set of measures, the 'what' we want to accomplish. Just as the outcome lists held emergent patterns which prompted the measures, the action lists hold emergent patterns which comprise a much optimised version of our 'Go!' step. We have been transforming that single, starting effort into a set of related moves which have a far greater propensity to raise the scores of our most critical measures.

Review all the entries you have made in action spaces. Once you defined first outcomes, both best and worst, all further statements of action you made were re-actions to whatever outcomes you stated. The statements were elaborations of the 'Go!' action which got the entire process started. In a sense these actions are children of the original step, because they occurred as a result of the range of possibility made possible by the 'Go!' step. They include suggestions of what we-knew-but-didn't-know-we-knew about what our path must include to get optimal outcomes right from the beginning.

Patterns of 'Act to Recover' steps provide the foundation for assuring that the measures reach and exceed minimum acceptable levels. Do these without fail.

Patterns of 'Act to Enhance' entries will serve your longer range, ideal objectives and set the stage for superior achievement, pushing the measures well into the green zone.

Commonalities shared by both enhancement and recovery steps may well occur. Patterns may suggest novel sequences of actions. If any action appears twice or more, consider it a must-do.

The actions material has been derived from over the learning edge. Some steps may seem a bit out of place, early, scary, or disconcerting. Examine these carefully and take time to ponder, explore and experiment for they are near or just beyond your own inner boundaries of experience. These stretches are the essence of individual and organisational learning.

When the patterns are formed, restate them as if they were a new 'Go!' statement. This is a good time to rearrange things. The emergent actions are now in service of the measured objectives. The cases and the data sets have done their work. We have a better idea of what we are after and a more robust action set to get started.

Road Testing

Now, we can take each of the emergent actions and test it for impact on every measure. For any action against any measure, will the condition of the measure go up or down from where it is now? Will there be any effect? This is just a sanity check to make sure that we are not creating another worst-case outcome that we didn't think of previously. In general, there won't be a problem. Or, if there is, it is easily corrected in some adjustment of the action. Do this for every action against every measure.

Going Further with Implemento

For an even richer Implemento conversation the process can be repeated to incorporate a second round of scenario building to gather more insights. After the first round, and before processing the conversation, go through the conversational process again. In other words, start from the assumption that you have implemented the acts to enhance from the first round and more of the best happens. Lightning really does strike twice!

We pushed for the best and we got it, achieving more of the best results we can imagine. Write these results in a new 'Best Outcomes' domain. Then. Wow. If ever there was a time for bold, creative action then surely it is now and we can describe these in a second 'Acts to Enhance' domain. We've created a 'Best-Best' case.

A 'Best-Worst' case builds on the initial acts to enhance, but in this case our actions result in some worst-case outcomes and that sinking feeling needs further acts to recover.

A third case explores the 'Worst-Best' and, whew, we must have done some things right as best results turn up as an outcome of our initial recovery actions. Take the chance to build on these with new actions to make the most of these new best outcomes – capture these in a third 'Acts to Enhance' domain.

Finally a 'Worst-Worst' case – just when we thought things had gotten as bad as they could have, they get worse! This third 'Worst Outcomes' domain needs another set of acts to recover as there is nowhere to go but up! It might be to run away … maybe a bold step… maybe… who knows! Write these actions to rebuild the situation towards a more satisfying outcome in the final 'Acts to Recover' domain.

This is simply an extension of the initial conversation, pushing us further into speculation, imagination, out of our normal patterns of thinking, over the learning edge. We process the results in exactly the same way as described earlier. But now we have three sets of data for each domain – best outcomes, worst outcomes, acts to enhance, acts to recover – rather than just one. Treat them all simply as data, not distinct elements, part of the same conversation. Look for the patterns. I like to start with the 'Acts to Recover' list so I am formulating foundation actions first. Once I have that set patterned I review the 'Acts to Enhance' data. Often I can make linkages from the new materials into some of the existing patterns. And I usually find a new integration or two or three. It takes some play to find novel integrations. I like putting opposites together best and finding how something novel will emerge in my imagination from the collision. If you have the time and the headspace for this longer process you may be surprised and will certainly be rewarded.

Implemento in Context

Implemento is the prospective method of the Stucco-Implemento pair. I use Implemento in order to get a far better understanding of the critical measures of success and to get a positive start on building measures and trying out some ventures. When we have established the measure which is the most critical and has a low score we have a starting point for Stucco. We ask ourselves, "What is it that constrains us from raising that score halfway to the max?"

The answer to that is a set of conditions that exist in the system. Stucco begins there and works retrospectively, back in time, to uncover root causes of the mess. Stucco uses the ideals and must-haves developed with Implemento and suggests new actions of its own. I alternate Stucco and Implemento in a continuing series of exploring back and testing forward until inoperative assumptions are revealed, break down and new ones are invented and tested. Somewhere along the line, the root cause of the mess becomes evident. Alternative behaviours are already in practice and commitment begins to take over from possibility.

After Implemento we move then to Impacto, which organises a compelling story for enrolling other stakeholders into whatever changes are being made.

Impacto

Impacto is related to the 'Influence' domain on the Insight Cycle. Some of the forces in play in the landscape of our endeavour, like the weather or gravity, are not susceptible to our control. But some of the most important Influences are people and we can certainly work with them. Impacto helps to frame a story about our actions and intentions that will enrol the people who can influence our success - either with their active support or simply by promising a fair wind or even getting out of the way.

Schemes, dreams, plans, goals, changes and everything else we do require other people to lead, follow or get out of the way. Each of us runs into the puzzle of how best to communicate a tough message to someone important in our lives. How to bring about the most understanding in the shortest time? How to create allies instead of sceptics and enemies? How to gain others' best thinking about the challenge at hand? How to ensure sustainable support? How to be in charge of the communication, however charged? How to test for the others' understanding? When to go faster or slower?

Impacto is our offering to aid with these challenges. It is a process map with five domains: Purpose, Urgency, Destination, Success Path and Commitment. Each domain is a necessary part of a communication which lets others know what we are up to and why and how we want them involved or not involved.

Impacto is both a framework for thinking and a design and delivery process for communications which enrols people in our cause. It gives us a way to develop understanding in the other person, layer by layer. It gives us frequent, natural opportunities to stop and assess whether common understanding and agreement is developing. To go no faster or further than the other person is prepared to go. It gives us a plan for orderly retreat if we have overstepped the other person's ability to hear us. It puts us in charge of the process. It builds allies. It is strategic enough to communicate upward. In fact, it is essential preparation for anyone seeking support from higher organisational levels.

The Domains

Rarely does anyone begin Impacto at the beginning and go to the end, filling in the blanks. Each domain is deeply interlinked with the others. An addition or modification in one will ripple through the others. The design process may well be jazzy, meandering, helter skelter, a free for all. Eventually, a story will reveal itself on the map. Larger threads appear. The domains align themselves. This can take an hour or a day or two, depending on the complexity of the issue and the clarity of your purposes.

To get started, find the domains where you feel you have some material, some interest, and some energy to state the case. Put down whatever you have. Emptied of this, take a stab at a domain which remains thin or empty. At the invention stage, do not concern yourself with how well the story hangs together. It's more important simply to get everything you believe you know and want on the map.

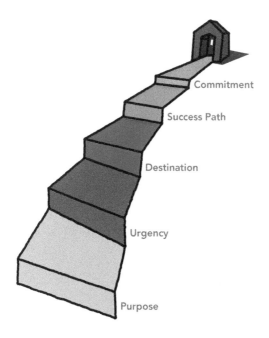

Purpose

Our purposes give a foundation of meaning to the rest of the communication. Good people do not get enrolled when purposes are fuzzy or wavering. The hows and whats and whens will vary and change dynamically. Purposes are the steadying forces which sustain us in the changes. The following questions should prompt the right kind of content in the 'Purpose' section of Impacto:

- What motivates you to invest your time and energy in this idea?
- Where does this effort fit with other things that are important to you?
- What is your highest intention?

Urgency

What is driving us to do something? What is the context, the situation, the conditions and forces which conspire to get us moving? Urgency is made up of opportunity, threats and risks, and the limits or richness of our powers.

- What strengths do you have that are not being fully used?
- What is missing that is needed?
- What is the opportunity – when does it begin and when does it end?
- What risks/threats do you face by doing nothing?

Destination

We and our compatriots require an aligned and mutually appealing view of how the world will look once changed by our combined efforts. Acting purely out of urgency may cause reactive, uncoordinated movement if we do not have a destination in mind. Our purpose is not a destination. We seek a vibrant, pragmatic and compelling set of outcomes to shoot for.

- What does 'good' look like?
- What do you want existing good things to evolve into?
- What changes in the world do you want to contribute to?

Success Path

We have our starting place defined and we have stated a destination. Now for the set of stepping stones which will mark our progress to the destination. This may be stated as a strategy or as a plan of events. It will describe how the story of success unfolds over time.

- How can you get from your current situation to your destination?
- What changes are necessary to move forward?
- Suppose you are standing in the future with your outcomes fully achieved. Looking back in time, what did you and others do to get here from there?

Commitment

Finally we describe the pragmatic reality of our personal commitment. What we are setting forth is not just an idea or a possibility, it is real, happening and underway. We are invested, personally. We can define what we are already doing and what our near-term actions are. Make a statement about what you can be relied on for. As well, we ask for discrete, measurable actions and contributions from the others, from money and resources to personal values.

- What matters to you?
- What contribution can you be relied upon to make?
- What requests are you making of others?
- How can other people increase the chances of success?

Telling the Impacto Story

When we communicate with Impacto we use a strict sequence, following the steps on the map. This is the key to building layers of understanding, agreement and commitment between ourself and the others. We state each domain briefly, then listen and inquire for the audience's understanding and recognition of the truths of our offering. The move from one domain to another offers a natural place to pause and check the level of agreement and understanding in the audience. And to listen!

Usually, the audience knows things we do not. Or they have differing frameworks of thinking which we can integrate into our Impacto map.

> *A computer systems staff group was trying to gain approval to spend $50 million on research, design and equipment. They went in to the CEO with a hard hitting story about the technical geewhizzery which they all understood and believed in. The CEO didn't get it. So, they didn't get it.*

Purpose. If they don't share our purposes, the audience can never buy or may never even see the rest of our work. If they cannot 'hear' our purposes, it means we do not understand their purposes and needs. Once unveiled, our work is a shared creation. Every step of the way demands our effort to find a framework of thinking which aligns us and them.

Urgency. Once everyone is nodding their heads 'yes' to purpose, we can go on to the urgency. Urgency speaks to people in both facts and feelings.

> *As he moved from urgency to destination, John began to invite input from the others. He put some 'bones' on the wall as a rough skeleton for his outcomes. He asked the others for the meat by leading a conversation about the bones. By the time he got to the success path, the others were adding to it, tossing in good and not so good ideas and were clearly enrolled in the project. They had become allies and fellow travellers. As he moved on to steps ahead, he had a room full of volunteers.*

The facts bring awareness that something must change. The feelings bring anger, excitement, action; a kind of human airspeed which gets things moving. As soon as people's speed is up, they will want some direction.

Destination. Describing outcomes requires people to do extra work in their minds to see the future. Building on the airspeed from the urgency, we often have spare energy available based on good reasons to go somewhere new. These outcomes reflect our highest purposes and speak to a resolution of the urgencies while engaging the audience in the fruitful possibilities of such a future.

Success Path. Now we come to the place most people mistakenly want to begin the conversation: the how-tos. The success path is next to last because talking about how to get something done is irrelevant if people are not agreed on purpose, urgency and outcomes.

Commitment. Given everything to this point, people want to know our commitment and level of effort. People want ideas about how they can proceed in the near term and have a hand in interesting, success oriented, strategically important projects. With the foundation in place it is easier to ask them for needed contributions. Enrolled, they will usually volunteer something. By this time there is no selling to do. They sold themselves somewhere back in the process. We don't really care where.

At any point in the process, we can stop. If people are not agreed we can acknowledge the disagreement and refuse to go further. We might sketch the rest to close it and let it hang for a while. If one segment does not go well, we can stop and explore what is true for everyone before proceeding. Even if we do not proceed at all that day, there will be another day.

> *Joanne spelled out her purposes to the Marketing Director and his staff. She thought of this part as a warm-up to the really good stuff contained in the destination and success path.*

> *The Director, nodding affirmatively through the purposes, looked stunned and quizzical as Joanne launched into the urgencies.*

> *Joanne stopped. She started over with urgency, simply stating the areas of urgency she had to discuss: competitors, cost of financing, customer concerns and morale in engineering. She asked the Director and staff to share their view of those forces.*

> *The Director led a 15-minute discussion which clarified the staff's view of the morale issue. By now, time was up for Joanne.*

> *She never delivered the rest. But, with agreement on the purposes and deeper insight into the morale question, she charged on ahead, enjoying the staff 's collaborative support, doing exactly what she had originally tried to persuade the Director to support.*

If the others cannot hear us, they will not hear us. Either we or they or both need to do some work to bring ourselves into alignment. Into common language. Into shared interests. Then and only then, can we attempt the next steps of the enrolment dance.

Impacto can be used by itself or as a part of a larger system of work. It organises a compelling story for enrolling other stakeholders into whatever changes are being made. The Impacto story either goes together or it does not. If not, we back up and continue the Stucco-Implemento loop. Otherwise we get on with life and come back at a later time to start over. A more desirable situation may have emerged by then, and it is very likely that our aspirations will have increased as the original dispiriting mess gets cleared up.

However you proceed with Impacto, my best wishes for great good fortune, inspiring purposes, marvellous success paths, and enduring commitments.

TransforMAP

The TransforMAP relates to the 'Mind' domain of the Insight Cycle. This is where our consciousness, culture, worldview, psychological response, assumptions and beliefs come into play. As mentioned earlier, these are always at the core of whatever mess we find ourselves in. TransforMAP brings them to awareness and offers the opportunity to intervene effectively at this point in the Cycle.

The TransforMAP is a guide for making headway through the uncertainty, confusing feelings and conflicting thoughts which accompany significant change. With your material added, the map reflects a story to you about what is really changing, where you stand on the path, and what you might expect to discover next from within yourself.

The TransforMAP is a reflection for this time of our journey from one frame of mind and condition to another. Whether we are learning, changing our minds, restructuring things, living in high uncertainty, whether driven from inside us or driven by conditions in our world, the TransforMAP offers a path to raising our knowledge of who we are and where we are on the path. With rising awareness and structure comes the natural stimulus to finish what needs to be finished in our life and work. To explore what is calling to be unfolded. To invest in purposeful targets when it is time.

The map is scalable. It works for the momentary dislocations and the colossal life changing events. I lost my car keys along with the bright key ring I purchased in Denmark. Meanwhile, our close friends lost their two-year-old child in a stupid, unbelievable accident. Mine was a twenty-minute loss. A minor suffering. But with doses of anger, frustration, blaming, self-righteousness, self-blame, the felt absence of something which brought a bit of meaning, identity and joy to my life. Our friend's loss took at least five years of letting go, and there will be a lifetime of grappling with this forfeit of innocent life. A colossal suffering. Immeasurably different in dimension and time from mine.

That said, the two are, operationally, little different in the process necessary to hear and organise the voices, learn and move beyond the suffering, reinvent our lives and focus on living out our fervent intentions beyond the endings.

The map is non-judgemental. Whatever comes up has a place to fit and a positive reason to be there. Everything is helpful because everything is real. There are no 'bad' or 'good' voices. Just voices.

Who needs it? When, individually or in teams, we are caught up in the struggle with a transition, the map takes all the feelings and thoughts and activity and gives each a place to rest. It all fits. It can all make a kind of procedural sense, even though it is all happening at once and may seem wildly contradictory. Working with the map removes the bewilderment factor and points out the real work of hearing, exhausting and completing each stage of the change. And the map gives us some sense of progress in our transition across time.

For those facing a change in the future, the map is a great planning and awareness tool. The map predicts the type of material which will come from ourselves and others when the change hits. We also remember the processes of past changes and learn what our natural responses are so we know them when they reappear.

For those leading a change, the map is predictive of what to expect and helps the leader:

- locate where he or she is in the process
- move along as quickly as possible
- develop empathic personal stories
- appreciate the dilemmas of those who have not yet engaged the change
- develop a creative communications plan for the whole system.

This chapter, along with the background story in the appendix about TransforMAP's development, is a starting place to understand how this framework can be used effectively with ourselves or in conversations with another person or a group in times of change and transition, reducing waste and angst, building spirit and vitality, helping to move business and lives along.

Three Voices of Change

When we have a sense that things are changing, it is generally worth exploring what we mean by that. Over the years, in my experience, thousands of answers to that question have seemed to emanate from three different and very distinct 'Voices': a voice of endings full of fear and angst, a voice of reinvention full of energy and exploration, and a voice of commitment full of passion, intention and the disciplines of achievement.

All three voices are at work at once, as if three different people are talking inside our head. Hence the regular confusion and uncertainty during times of change. Each voice has a particular language and an affect associated with it, comprising three domains: feelings, thoughts and actions. Put more simply: heart, head and feet.

At any time, one voice is likely to be dominant. While there is an overall sequence, we are wherever we are at any moment. The TransforMAP conversation may be entered wherever your interest or feeling or need demands.

Voice 1: Ending

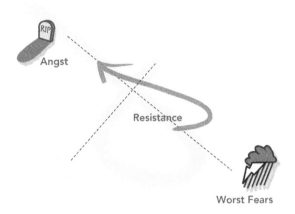

The voice of Ending has the ring of fear, sadness, anger, despair throughout. "I can't …" "We never …" "I'll be stuck forever!" This is the voice of the gottas, musts, nevers, always, shoulds, have tos, labels and judgements about self and others, the voice of doom, gloom and losing out, with stories of persecutors, victims and rescuers. In a change, we suffer. We feel an ending, a rip-off, as if a burglar has been in our bedroom while we were there, but asleep. We aren't sure what has been taken. We feel violated. Life will never again be quite as naive or simple. We are angry, sad, despairing, afraid, apprehensive.

Our head, responding to our feelings, goes to work predicting our future by imagining a set of dire consequences; a wake-up call about what may be occurring. Our mind becomes a cinema of worst fears. Given the feelings and fear-full imaginings, our feet start moving to resist the change, to avoid the consequences, to regain what we feel we are losing. We may hold on too long, deny our feelings and thoughts, and struggle to go back, away from the direction of change. If we are unwilling to let go, and continually try to recreate history, we ensure the realisation of our worst fears.

Letting go of what has ended and heading toward our fears,

rather than heading back, away from them, may take minutes or years. We acknowledge the loss. Say goodbyes and bury the dead. Honour all the ways they have been meaningful in our lives. As teachers, partners, possessions, good friends or valuable enemies. We create and do rituals to make it clear to every cell in our bodies that whatever was is no longer possible. We examine the worst fears to de-mystify them and find the essential stuff of the past to be valued in new ways in the future. What seems so distasteful or scary usually dissolves into misunderstanding or the results of limited information or old mythology left around from childhood. True, there are cautionary wisdoms within the fears, but nothing to stop us cold or drive us away in helpless reaction. Eventually then, we turn to consider what's next, what's possible, what can be learned through this, and how to lighten our load.

Voice 2: Reinvention

Successful designers continually sell or get rid of their best work, if they are to move on to truly new ideas. They are consummate explorers and learners. They live with faith that they can discover and realise an, as yet, fuzzy and emerging possibility. They take initiatives which promote learning, make some headway and bring the possibilities into clearer view. They act to unfold the possibility to provide a best set of credible choices. There is a voice of the explorer in the middle of us and at the middle of any transition. The voice of no longer needing everything of the past, of burial and release of the old, of wondering, blue-skying, making it up, of taking a flyer, taking a chance, and experimenting. Of persevering into a possibility. Our voice of Reinvention, as with each voice, begins with feelings. In Voice 1 we sought to finish outworn relationships, stuff, ideas, patterns of thinking, feeling and acting. These artefacts of the past naturally fall into the chronicles of our history which accomplishes at least two things. First, they are released by us, we break and finish our attachment to them, ending the suffering of Voice 1. Second, whatever has been ended no longer requires any of our attention or energy. This energy and attention is now available for something else. What we have felt as a loss in Voice 1 is now gone from our burdens and our body feels lighter, more free, we feel a release.

Unshackled from elements of the past, our mind's eye lifts skyward, toward the mountain's misty peaks, toward the vast, unexplored range of life's possibilities which have been existing, just out of view, beyond the safe boundaries of our past life habits, our old status quo, now in transition. Our feet set to work exploring, setting up temporary learning structures, meeting new people, speaking new ideas, wearing different colours, listening to a new music, and having a good, satisfying cry at a movie we would have never even considered watching only two weeks ago. As we explore possibilities and focus our interests we form increasingly concrete choices. A harmonious balance is struck between what is possible and our energy, resources and interest. A direction begins to coalesce. It is as if we have climbed the mountain of possibility, standing at the top with a new store of potential energy and direction. With just one step we enter the next turn on the map.

Voice 3 : Commitment

Passion   Discipline   Intention

Voice 3 speaks of passionate choice, direction, focus, discipline, and pragmatism. The fervour, resolve, exhilaration and creative danger run high. The man says "Place your bets!" Or, "Start your engines!" The time is now. We have let go of the old ways by completing Voice 1. We exhaustively explored the possibilities for us and created some powerful choices in Voice 2. We are now taking the intellectual, emotional and physical decision to turn our new, challenging intention into our real world.

We've mortgaged the house, hired twenty new folks, are seated on the edge of our chair with our special fountain pen in our hand, the one we save just for the really big deals. The person on the other side of the table slides the contract towards us with the huge red 'X' where our signature goes. We have arrived at clarity of purpose, a new perspective of our power and fortunes in the world. Our emotions express resolve, a centre, a focus. Our mind is engaged with a palpable, valuable intention. Our hands are busy constructing disciplines: the plans, procedures and methods necessary to protect and nurture our investment, and to interact with the forces in the world to give us the best probability of living out our intentions.

Voice 3 expresses commitment, hard currency, specific plans, spending the money, nailing things down, getting things in place, refining methods, delivering the bacon, making the goals, winning the contest and seeing our commitments through. Here we make the integration of our learning complete. We commit, do it, see it through, take the heat, learn hard lessons, and deliver something out of our life efforts and the time spent. We are expanded, richer in knowledge and wider in perspective than when we began our journey all the way back in Voice 1. Learning is completed and we have arrived at the beginnings of a new status quo.

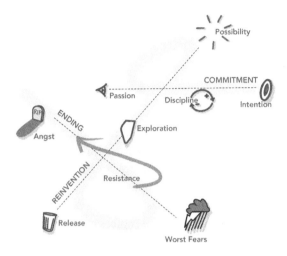

Voice 1: Ending – Domains

Angst

The heart in Voice 1. Which comes first, the apprehension of loss or the actual loss? The fear of what will happen if we lose something or the direct experience of life without something we value? Surely the feelings come before the actual living with. Our bodies speak in physical sensations. If

we sense a loss, we have sensations about it. Sensations are like file folders in the body. Each folder represents a specific set of body experiences like cold, clammy hands or a sinking feeling in the stomach. This feelings folder holds the memories of every life experience we have had when that feeling has been happening in our body. The feelings of change, sweeping through our body, bring all those memories into play, just beneath our awareness, but above our perception. The memories get repeated, reinforcing the heartfelt sensations. Indeed, something intangible, out at the edge of our awareness, is missing. Our body 'smells' a hardship, however subtle. A distress emerges of not knowing the dimensions of the thing. We 'feel' it as a body sensation. Then our mind makes an interpretation, based on past experience, and we name the feeling. Sadness isn't really a sensation, it is a sentiment which includes the sensation and an interpretation. Making this distinction between sensation and sentiment will be useful to us in helping ourselves reduce wasted angst and move along on the path of transition.

"I'm lost."

"I'm hot headed."

"My mouth is dry and my neck is stiff every day!"

What is to be done with this first assault of change, this sensation from the loss, this ending? First, and above all, we acknowledge all the feelings as they come along. They won't all happen at once. Sadness gives way to rage which gives way to frustration which gives way to an empty heart which gives way to an odd laughter and unstoppable tears at the mention of kayaking, or a name, or the sound of a long forgotten melody. No rhyme or reason. Just process. No need to make sense. Just be there. Listen. The only difference between listening to rage or listening to tears is to have something safe to hit for the rage and a box of tissues around for the tears.

Next, within each feeling we ask for the specific sensations, separating them from our sentiments and interpretations. Keep it coming, until it just stops one day of its own stopping. We do not deal with angst exclusively. Life has beginnings along with the endings. Airing the feelings in a balanced way along with the other domains in the TransforMAP will keep the finishing going. It will take its own bittersweet time. The toughest role for us is to just be there. Commiserating is bad form. Offering a tissue for damp eyes and sitting quietly is better than a hug. Remembering times of our own agony in transition brings empathy, not sympathy, and reminds us of the need to be humble and patient.

Particularly with this domain of the heart in the voice of Ending we need to pay attention to my earlier guidance (starting p.27) about supporting transition. I suggested we might offer three levels of support: problem-solving, transformative inquiry and presence. Given the nature of this part of the work we especially need to be practising inquiry and being present. We must proceed sensitively with an appreciation of the territory that is emerging before us. Enduring, unremitting or apparently destructive grief or rage, for example, whilst clearly part of the voice of ending, demands a resource of a different order, a professional therapist, someone skilled and experienced in human relations work, or even a doctor. These may be deep waters and it helps to remain aware.

Opening Lines

- What do you stand to lose as a result of the changes taking place?
- What do you feel is being taken away from you?
- Where does it hurt?
- How do you feel these days?
- Have you experienced this feeling before associated with a change?
- What is missing from your life as a result of the change?

Worst Fears

The head in Voice 1. We have warning systems in our bodies which inform us when the status quo is being interrupted.

Our homeostasis system attempts to maintain a steady balance in our bodies. Change is a challenge to that system. Our immune system starts acting up when the suffering begins. Therefore, we are prone to projecting our future as an exaggerated re-

construction of what has happened to us in the past, organised by the events and experience which the feelings bring with them. We have night-dreams and day-dreams. These produce nightmares, boogie monsters and other phantasms to get our attention, wake us up, cause us to take charge of things. If we take these literally, we can scare the hell out of ourselves. Individuals usually describe their worst imaginings in absolute terms as part of a dire story of a fruitless dark spiral of a future. We go wrong when we take these imaginings at face value and start acting on them as true and given. These are warning shots from the subconscious rather than torpedoes in the hull. But they look real and are there for a very good reason – they encase the cautionary wisdoms from life experience. Guards standing at the gate of change making up scary stories to stop us passing through.

"We'll never get there, we are headed for an absolute, unmitigated, all-singing, all-dancing DISASTER!"

"There is no light at the end of this tunnel"

"I always wind up out in the cold"

"You gotta live with what the boss says"

Some effort is required to get the value here. The imaginings and the resulting feelings often mask the voice of quality experience and reason. What seems best is to apply reason to the uggabuggas and 'de-mystify' them (see the work on completing the voices later in this section).

Opening Lines

- What are you thinking about these days?
- Does this bring up thoughts from the past?
- What's the worst that could happen?

Resistance

The feet in Voice 1. Our worst imaginings and the suffering that comes with them have tremendous power. The most dire contests in our lives will be between our will and our fears. When we resist the changes, reacting to our fears, and we all do at times, we go away from them, back

from the edge, towards previously safe and predictable conditions and people. Even if previous times were painful, we may take those over the unknown, or that predicted by our body in the face of a loss. We can spend years and fortunes attempting to recover past safety, avoiding the unknown.

Once we have a picture of our dire future projections, we can look at history to determine how we have previously behaved to avoid them. This inquiry often reveals a pattern. Once we are aware of the pattern, we can choose not to repeat it in the present transition. When we look at history the pattern most often tells a story of great attempts and unsustainable results. The resistance loop includes both denial and avoidance. It expends much energy, feels easier than confronting our worst projections and will not ever truly recover the past. Maybe for a moment. But not for long.

An example. A company no longer really needs a particular job to be done. The jobholder fears living without an income. He fears separation from the company which has become his family. Loneliness. Poverty. Destitution. Skid Row. Failure in the eyes of family. These extreme images are all attached to the feelings which the thought of the end of the job bring up. To avoid the imagined dark possibilities, the employee sets out to make himself indispensable, a pattern which has been going on since childhood. At seven years old, during the separation of his parents, he clung to Mum and became her little helper, doing every chore he could to stay in favour. At thirteen, upon learning that his mother was moving to another city, he got involved in every possible school and community activity to work the magic again and avoid a separation and the need to start relationships over again. Mother still moved and he did too. Albeit painfully. At twenty-six, at the beginnings of his own divorce, he heard himself say:

"I'll do everything and anything to stay here with you"

She still walked away. Now, at forty-three, he'll do anything to stay in the job. Of course, the job will go and so will he.

Opening Lines

- What do you find yourself doing these days?
- Is what you are doing now taking you towards greater life possibilities? Or more constrained safety? Towards what?
- How is this situation apparently like others in your life up to now?
- How have you dealt with the previous situations?
- What are you doing to deal with your worst fears?

Voice 2: Reinvention – Domains

Release

The heart in Voice 2. Resolution of our losses, facing up to our suffering and choosing to stay engaged with our transition rather than run away has been called 'dying to the situation'. The feeling that unfolds immediately after such a surrender is one of relief and lightness. We have set down a burden. The ultimate burden,  of course, is letting go of our physical life. The literature on death and dying describes the blissful state that some people gain when they are dying and pass the point of holding on in their physical form.

The other side of an ending is a new freedom. While we could view it as something lost from a Voice 1 perspective, we see it as un-shouldering a burden in Voice 2. Whatever we have 'lost' is, in some way, no longer any use to us. For example, I am free to find another key ring. My friend's child's room gets redecorated, it is no longer his room. Anything that puts us back in Voice 1 can be given away, renegotiated, reinvented. We recycle it all into more fundamental energy for other activities. Release lets go of the emotional burdens of the old order, setting us free to lighten up.

"Funny. Here I am in the middle of this big change and I feel almost giddy. I'm excited and scared at the same time."

These feelings are just about the complete opposite of those found in Voice 1. Voice 1 is oppressive, depressive, crazy making. The heart in Voice 2 is uplifted, light, soaring, excited, enthusiastic, wonder-full, optimistic, dancing, and so on.

Opening Lines

- What no longer works?
- What do you keep in your life that is an impediment to new possibilities?
- What do you keep that is a reminder of past problems?
- What could you give up for now that would enable you to experiment with new ideas?

Possibility

The head in Voice 2. Changes, no matter how dreary or limiting they may appear, actually take the lid off the possibility container. The rules are changing, conditions are changing, all things are in flux. Surely unstable times have dangers. They equally have opportunities. The  most common failure to make something of a change comes when people spend most of their time avoiding the perceived dangers and little time building possibilities. As fears are demystified, avoidance patterns seen for what they are and the losses sufficiently mourned and laid to rest, people's natural energy shifts towards determining what they can make of the situation they are now in. We've had good luck asking the possibility question right at the outset without dwelling on it until the person's frame of mind naturally turns toward design of a new life.

"I had a thought ... maybe coaching kids through their adolescence is a great possibility for me!"

Using our head to dream up new possible lives to live is important work. We are going to make a claim on the future. We are going to put who we already are together with some new components, not yet defined, to create a new person in a new context with a new perspective. So we need to give time to making up new scenarios and constellations of who we are for the future.

Opening Lines

- What's the best that could happen now?
- What would be perfect for you and you alone?
- What would be an exceptional life, work, relationship, house, child, or community for you?
- Assume you are living in the best possible world for you. What are the components of this ideal situation?

Exploration

The feet in Voice 2. Possibilities are often large and fuzzy. We need to explore them until they focus and simplify into clearer goals and purposes. Possibilities provide the focus for making new, active explorations. Knowing how we avoided old fears keeps us from wasting those actions on avoiding ourselves. Knowing what we have left in the past keeps us from reinvesting energy in activities which return us nothing.

People usually make smallish learning experiments at first, when the unknowing is rather high. Using the mountain metaphor, if we are climbing, uncovering the path as we go, we must make some excursions and suffer some dead ends if we expect to develop a quality route to the summit. We cannot be sure of each immediate outcome. We don't want to limit ourselves by prematurely committing to more than we can handle and what is not right for us. We have limited energy and we want it expended in the service of our possibilities.

"I'm researching all the ways that single people meet and share time with others once they are over fifty."

The natural outcome of a solid time of exploration is a genuine sense of passionate direction for the future. And within that direction are some well understood choices to make.

Opening Lines

- What are the first five things you can think of to start learning about the possibilities you see?
- Suppose you were a person who was moving powerfully through this change. What would you be doing now?
- Where can you go to find out more?

Voice 3: Commitment – Domains

Passion

The heart in Voice 3. Passion is the word I use to collect the feelings that come with Voice 3. Passion does not describe our choice, but how it feels to have a fire in our belly, be aligned, and committed. The tone of Voice 3 is energised, sure-footed, resolute, directed, firm, crisp and definite.

"I feel so solid, so fired up, so clear and I'm scared out of my wits. It's just great."

This is the nature of the turn from Reinvention to Commitment. We have learned a lot as we imagined all the possibilities and made our learning explorations. In time our head, heart and feet get aligned and the passion for a new journey rises. We make the 'place your bets' commitment, put our eye on a specific intention and move on into our new life.

Opening Lines

- On a scale of one to ten, how confident do you feel of what is to come?
- When you look forward, what feelings arise?
- What's your level of energy for the objective you've set?
- What are you really committed to in all of this?
- How do you feel about where you are headed?
- What decisions have you personally started taking in order to get going?

Intention

The head in Voice 3. Intentions are specific, concrete aspirations, prizes and targets which form through the transition process and which inspire tough, direct action. Intention is unambiguous in purpose, values, quality, and style. Intention has a ring of deeply felt truth about it. It makes logical sense to us. We light up when we talk about our  intention. A creative voice emerges which works tirelessly to find ever better ways to live out our intent. Strong intentions generate an energetic spiral drawing us into ever tighter focus and commitment.

"I'm seeing to it that kids in our community have a new chance for an alternative education."

Opening Lines

- What are your targets?
- What is the real purpose behind this change?
- What is this transition leading to in terms of new outcomes?
- What can we now achieve?
- Our entire history has brought us past a point of decision, into commitment to a new future. What is that new future we are creating?

Discipline

The feet in Voice 3. Our hands and feet get going in Voice 3. Given a commitment of resources to a particular direction, we naturally create structures, rules of play and disciplines which give us the best chance of succeeding. Our intention grows  brighter as we implement and improve our disciplines. We want to limit the risk to our investment and raise the favourable odds of living out our intention. We want to ensure that our lifetime is usefully spent. We set accounting rules in our businesses. We structure how we're going to get the diapers washed and keep adequate inventory in the right place at the right times. We make time schedules, choose specific ways to discuss issues with our associates, clients, suppliers. We establish rituals of our work clothing. We hold to maintenance routines for devices we trust to keep us alive and well as we journey from Jakarta to Des Moines. We hold effective meetings, take care with what we write and communicate, plan carefully and generally do our work, from chopping wood and carrying water to running the country, with passion, dedication, curiosity, joy and care.

"Let me show you the plan, the rules we're going to play by, and the way we're going to measure our place and progress."

In short, we construct and operate good disciplines – dynamic, resilient and smart systems derived from the creative need to respond to an ever-changing environment and to the growing richness of our intent. These activities are not resistance lurking in Voice 1. They are not hidebound rules which come from fear, nor are they unsustainable habits of the past. These disciplines are worthwhile allies on our intent-full journey. We hear them spoken, in Voice 3, in positive and energetic terms, as helpers and optimistic paths to an end.

Opening Lines

- What are you spending your time doing?
- Tell me about structures you have put in place?
- Let's talk about the new rules of the game
- What do we need to do to avoid risks becoming reality?
- What will it take to get this done?
- How will we know we're on track?

Ways of Working with TransforMAP

I see TransforMAP as a framework for self-awareness. It can also be used to guide an informal conversation. It can be a helpful framework for working more rigorously both with individuals and with groups facing change. Each asks for different skills while both are based on exactly the same vocabulary and logical structure.

The opening to a TransforMAP session is usually the same. "What's changing?" is a great question to begin with. Or we could ask, "What's ending?" Or, "What's new?" And, "What are you getting after?" That covers the voices. We could start with heart, head, and feet. "How does it feel?" Or, "What are you thinking about?" Or, "What are you spending time doing?"

With these open questions and some rudimentary inquiry skills, following the domains of the map as a guide and following up on actions which suggest themselves, we can gently facilitate profound reductions in the time and angst of a change. We can increase the richness of meaning and understanding which a real change can bring, broaden the grasp of life's purposes and offerings, and promote getting on with the right and necessary actions instead of the apparently urgent and diversionary.

In casual conversation, people often reveal the frustration of a feeling or a worst fear; something provocative that we will hear in one of the three voices. A natural way to turn that input into a useful conversation is to pursue it, from our side, as a tour of the map.

I used to practise working with the map on long haul flights. Sitting next to someone over five or six hours usually led to a chat and more often or not something would come up about a challenge and a change. Rather than just make small talk and commiserate, which I was never very good at, I just took it upon myself to converse from the intelligence of the map and run the risk that the other person would go away with an insight or two which they didn't have when they boarded the plane.

My experience has been that with a sense of the TransforMAP, it is almost impossible to avoid being an interested, compassionate party who serves the evolution of the other party by simply listening and inquiring with the vocabulary and structure of the map.

This is not just about technique. Caring for another who is making passage through a life or work upheaval is a labour of the heart as well as the mind. There are no right answers. There is only patience, a listening viewpoint, and allowing time for the unfolding to take place. There is a willingness to sit with ambiguity, indecision and no idea of what to do next except wait to find what your heart suggests.

The next few pages offer some directions about how to work more rigorously with the TransforMAP. The first phase involves inquiring into the domains and integrating and telling the story back. You will most always complete this. The second phase moves the work from using the TransforMAP as a reflection and awareness process into the exhaustion and completion of the dominant voice, actively guiding individuals and/or groups through the process of transition.

Working with an Individual

First up I should say that I regard working formally with an individual as a contracted coach as a distinct form of engagement. It requires skills that are beyond the scope of this book – although support is available from my friends at Executive Arts for those wishing to gain those skills and use TransforMAP in this way. As noted above, in discussing the voice of endings in particular, a coaching conversation using the TransforMAP can lead an individual into personal depths that require a degree of experience and sensitivity (not to mention supervision) to manage safely and effectively.

What follows should therefore be read in the context of less formal conversation where you have a relationship with the individual but not a formal coaching contract. Where there is a basis of trust and, on your part, a willingness to be of service. And where you feel confident in the core practices of open listening and fair storymaking that I covered in the early part of this book. As a framework for self-awareness during change, the first individual TransforMAP conversation may be with yourself!

The first step in doing the work is to get the other person to tell their story of feelings, thoughts and actions in their own terms, with their own vocabulary. This first telling becomes the basis of the map. We may or may not use a printed map; we might just make it up on a blank sheet. They have told us their cover story for the change. It is true according to their perceptions and fits what they think they know about the situation and want us to know about it. Our job is to exhaust this surface knowing and open the door to something deeper which springs from their unknowing. We want to engage their learning edge.

Ultimately, as workers with the TransforMAP we have to be storytellers. And we want the richest source material we can have to build the stories with. So, we are interviewing our clients, if you will, well into their unknowing, where they can find more profound material for the story. Some of this will happen as we follow our curiosity around the map and ask them to tell us about domains which they have said little or nothing about. They will have to make something up, which may unlock a door to an insight they have not yet had. For the places where they do have material, I prefer to inquire into fuzzy words they use and simply ask what those words mean. We all use convenient shorthand and culturally popular words to describe what is true for us, even though those words are almost meaningless. No good journalist or writer would ever let those go. They dig in and find feeling, colour, nuance and specific meanings and images, as should we. Once we are satisfied that we have exhausted their perceptions and observations and experience, and have placed all their material on to the context of the map, we can tell the story as a flow from Voice 1 through to Voice 3.

Here we use the principles of fair storymaking. So, "I am a person who..." or "We are people who..." are places to begin. We tell the story in the first person, present tense. We are in Voice 1, Voice 2 and Voice 3 all at the same time. We hold these fears and feelings and work to avoid them. We have ideas about the possible future, and at times feel unburdened and are trying out new things. We have an intent in mind, feel resolute about it and are working to get on a success path to it. Or we don't. We have some or all or not much. That's the story. No need to make up what isn't there. It just isn't there. The story tends to rest in one of the voices as the dominant energy of this time.

Doing this a few times is a lot easier than explaining how to do it. You have the flow of voices to give you a story line. You have the heart, head and feet domains within each voice to give you a logic of feeling-drives-thinking-drives-action, or thinking-evokes-memory-evokes-feeling-evokes-action. You will find the way it works best for you. This completes a first phase and should satisfy the most basic of needs for the other person to become more fundamentally aware of themselves.

Working with a Group

Working with a group feels closer to regular facilitation, with the TransforMAP giving an underlying structure for the conversation.

One difference is that there is no need to find some sort of consensus view of the change across a group. A group should be considered as a collection of individuals rather than an entity for this work. There can be no real negotiation of where people are in the change. Some lead, some lag, some are all over the place. Some are here one day, there another. What's important in the process is to get everyone heard and their words on the map or on the walls in some way. A pattern will emerge that gives us a starting place to work from. There is no need for anyone to 'fit in' to a group position.

If we think of every person in the room as a walking, talking TransforMAP, each will have worst fears which exist in front of them down near the floor. The possibilities they perceive occur in front of them and above their head. And their intentions exist directly in front of their chest. Now imagine all of these map-droids, if you will, standing in a circle facing inward. The collection of their worst fears would be in the middle of the circle on the floor. The collection of possibilities in the centre above the group and the intentions in a cluster in the middle of the circle at chest level.

This stack of material in the centre is all of the *head-related domains* from the map. They are of the mind and so they offer us a reasonable, logical place to do group work. If nothing else, I want to make sure these three domains – from the voice of endings, reinvention and commitment – are fully explicit and everyone has a chance to be influenced by everyone else.

Emergent patterns in each domain are prime targets for pragmatic work to move the group through transition. Worst fears need to be de-mystified and transformed to possibility. Possibilities need to be extended and pushed beyond the learning edge and transformed into intention. Intentions need to be aligned, clarified and intensified.

As the worst fears let go and possibilities rise, angst and resistance behaviours naturally subside while release and explorations take their place. As intentions are shared, clarified and focused, the passion of the group to get going rises along with the disciplines of pragmatic achievement.

In summary, we get all the individual data mapped as best we can, making sure that we have an exhausted stack of worst fears, possibilities and intentions on the wall. Depending on the volume and intensity of the three different voices, we then spend time completing the most energetic voice.

Completion: Moving Through Transition

So far, inquiry and reflection will reveal a story of feelings, thoughts and actions that is the basis of the map. As we work with the TransforMAP we have to be storytellers and follow our curiosity around the domains until we have mapped all the material and integrated and have a story with colour, nuance, specific meanings and images which tells us, among other things, which of the voices is dominant at this time. We need to exhaust all perceptions, observations and experience.

What we may discover, whether we are working with an individual or a group, is that in practice they may be stuck in a voice or may want or need to speed up their transition process to the maximum speed they can go. If so, our job is to dig deeper into the dominant voice and release any unneeded reasons to stay there. And set some positive linkages in place from the dominant voice to the next one, so there is a natural tension evolving which will provide an energising place to go next.

Maximum speed here will seem almost glacial compared to what the business plan may intend. It is not glacial, but it will have to work in human time, even though we have removed most of the wasted time and angst and resource from the process.

While all the domains are in play in a change, there is a general movement from Voice 1 through to Voice 3, just as we tell the story. At any time, one voice will be dominant, taking centre stage. It is possible to get stuck in a voice. While I don't think that is likely to last forever, it can last so long that a good strategy is defeated, or the moment is lost, or we waste our resources pursuing resistance or experiments to the point that we have nothing left for the needed investment in Voice 3, when we finally do get there.

Change does require living through it and takes its own time, but not forever.

When the voices are positively activated and heard enthusiastically, the pace of the individual and the group from the endings to the creative bits can be remarkably rapid. Plenty of speed to keep everyone on their toes and important milestones reached. What do 'positive activation' and 'enthusiastic hearing' mean? Partly they mean just using the map and checking in with the heart, head and feet of each voice. When we activate a voice from a positive point of view and listen enthusiastically we are simply inquiring into each domain without judgement and with the optimistic view that with enough inquiry we will reveal new, helpful material and insight, further releasing the bindings to a particular voice or point of view which inhibit natural movement through the changes.

Completing an Ending

Most healthy people don't look forward to feeling poorly. And most organisations have cultural taboos about how much emotion can be displayed at work. Further, our overall cultural messages to one another about feeling and looking your best all the time through new clothes, face lifts and swell cars, strongly reinforce the belief that feelings of doubt, loss, fear and so on are things to be avoided or made to go away as soon as possible with the least effort, and the greatest consumption of goods and services.

The feelings of Voice 1 can be pretty overwhelming. All the way to the point of despair. Not to be trifled with. And certainly not to be suppressed or ignored. Pushing these natural and timely expressions back down into ourselves forces them to come out in other ways. Suppressed, they will attempt to come through our thinking – making our worst fears even more 'worst' – or come out through our hands and feet – putting our behaviour really over the top. If we can express the feeling directly we have one level of effect. If we have to force that expression out through another mode, it has to be done with an order of magnitude more effort to attempt to make the point.

By inquiring into the feelings as part of the mapping exercise we activate the witness in each of us who is not undergoing the feeling, but can notice and report on the experience. So we have one path to get the feelings out: talking to the witness. As we are not licensed psychologists, this is safe ground for us and safe for the people we interact with. "Please tell me about the feelings you are carrying now" is a good way to get started. Asking the witness for some measures about how much of the time the feelings have centre stage and how deeply these feelings run is also very useful to help them really perceive that who they are is not their feelings – the feelings just come around and are very present on occasion.

The notion of a feeling like 'sad' is quite a construct of mind. Asking 'what is sad?' is like asking 'what is the colour red?' or 'what is the flavour of vanilla ice cream?' 'Sad' is a shorthand to describe an integrated package of experience, mental models and body sensation. Every one of us constructs 'sadness' in our own way. For our purposes, the really factual stuff is the specific body sensations which come with our version of 'sad'. And this is the principal inquiry to demystify the feelings and complete them.

Ask where they occur in the physical body. Bring the witness's attention to this inquiry. Ask, "What is happening in your body that tells you that you are experiencing sadness?" Or, "When you are sad, where do you feel it in your body?" Or, "How do your feelings of sadness occur in your body?"

We ask for this specific evidence of feelings by going directly at the actual sensations rather than interpretations of sensations. This works nicely for individuals. When we work with groups we are looking for collective feelings. These occur as well. Situations really do feel 'hollow' or 'compressed', or 'up tight' or 'on fire' to groups. These kinds of words come directly from body sensations which numbers of people are experiencing and which can characterise the collective anxiety.

Burying the Dead

As we discover the outworn thinking, relationships, methods, policies, behaviours and values which need to be left to the past we can hold wakes, funerals, celebrations and burial ceremonies in order to lay the past to rest and be freer to move on. Resistance behaviour in the form of denial and avoidance is completely built on the belief that the world has not and will not really change. Public and private ceremonies which require preparation, viewing the body, putting caskets in the ground or on pyres are very impressive to our inner selves. They are all designed for those that must live on in a new world without that which has ended. Every culture has its forms of burying the dead. And all accomplish the same thing: set the living free to get on with the world, or, in our terms, complete Voice 1. Given our cultural norms, we can use these ceremonies in appropriate ways to complete whatever we must leave in the past. If we are abandoning an organisational structure for a new one, we could take a pile of existing drawings of the ending structure and burn them in the car park. On the count of three, we can each take one drawing, wad it up in a ball and toss it into the waste bin in the centre of the room, and keep tossing until we get them all in. This ritual for the 'dead' will serve us well.

Demystifying Worst Fears

Worst fears are imaginings, not realities. When we attempt to hide from them we bring them about. When we go at them we find they are full of holes and remarkably easy to cut down to their real size. In the previous section on Worst Fears I presented the following examples of how they sound absolute in Voice 1:

"We will never get there"

"There is no light at the end of this tunnel"

"I always wind up out in the cold"

"You gotta live with what the boss says"

To demystify these we inquire into the meaning of the absolute and fuzzy words in the statement:

"Do you 'always' wind up out in the cold?"

"Well not always."

"So, when have you wound up out there and when haven't you? How is this situation like the one or the other? How is it unlike either? What is really true now?"

"Tell me more about what being 'out in the cold' means to you."

We can dig deeper to find what the actual worst thing is that can happen:

"What's the worst that can happen?"

"I could lose my job."

"What would happen then?"

"I'd have to sell my house."

"Why?"

"Because I'd have no money."

"Is it true, you would have 'no' money?"

"Well, no. I have enough for three months."

"So what's the worst that could happen?"

"I'd run out of money before I could find another job."

"How could that actually happen?"

Demystifying includes testing all the 'you can'ts', 'you gottas', 'you nevers', 'you musts' and 'you anythings' which individuals use to describe their situation. We assume that every one of these is followed by an implied 'because' followed by a worst fear or limiting belief. For example

> *"You can't just go right up to the boss and tell him what you think!"*
>
> *"Because?"*
>
> *"People just don't do that."*
>
> *"Because?"*
>
> *"It just is not appropriate for the workplace."*
>
> *"Because?"*
>
> *"Because..."*
>
> *"Because why?"*
>
> *"Because I'm afraid he won't understand me."*
>
> *"So being understood is important to you? Please tell me more..."*

Did you notice how 'you' shifted to 'I' at the same time as the real fear surfaced? The word 'you' used with absolute words around it usually signals that we are hearing unrealistic, self-limiting beliefs that feed the fears. When I hear this, I ask the person to repeat the exact statement using 'I' instead of 'You'. This 'I'-based statement will sound two or three hundred percent over the top. And the speaker will usually make adjustments and repeat it immediately to get it back down to earth. The work is to stay with 'I' statements on the same topic until we reach a statement that sounds fair and right.

There is a natural shift that happens as we pursue this work with the worst fears. In a relatively short time the speaker will begin to use Voice 2 in the midst of the demystifications. Above we have the line:

> *"Because I'm afraid he won't understand me."*

As Voice 2 emerges we might hear a following line:

> *"Of course if I ever actually talked to the boss, he might have a chance to understand me."*

This is quite a shift. First it is not about the boss anymore, it is about the person's own responsibility. Second, they have opened the door to an experiment and a possibility. Experiment with actually talking to the boss and the possibility that the boss can actually hear if communicated with. Voice 1 has been transformed into Voice 2.

That is one way of saying it. Another is that Voice 1 is being completed. Underneath the imaginings of a fear construct was a reality about the speaker's choices so far. And with that, in a positive and enthusiastic context, comes the admission that the boss hasn't really had a chance yet. And neither has the speaker taken the chance.

For starters, we can positively inquire, without judgement, into the absolute terms of the stated worst fear. We don't need to be terrifically smart. Just ask for specificity. What does 'always' really mean in calendar time, for instance. And, of course, any other big, fuzzy words are fair game as well.

Demystifying Resistance

It is wildly tempting to make denial and avoidance behaviour wrong. It may be wrong in the eyes of the corporate thought police or even the real police. But in the spirit of actually moving past Voice 1 there is no value in making it wrong. This will be the real test in our ability to be fair, positive and enthusiastic. If our heads are off inventing worst fears, our hands and feet are most likely carrying us away from reality. The drive to avoid and resist change can be exceedingly strong. I do not suggest any attempts to actually arrest the hands and feet, the only entities which can do that are the hands and feet themselves. What we can do is to talk about and put real measures on the hows and wherefores of the resistance behaviour. Putting measures on behaviour is simply about defining how we will actually know how much of the behaviour is going on. A simple question is all that is needed: "How might I verify that this is happening?" Or, "How do you know when this is happening?"

In simple terms the answers will offer us at least three scales:

- Time: how much is spent
- Conditions: what conditions bring about the behaviour or come about as a result
- Actions: what we are actually doing, how we are actually behaving

A good set of measures raises our insight into what we are up to. That in itself is quite helpful because we have now become a witness to what may have been quite reactive, unconscious activity. We have set aside the captivation of our hands and feet by Voice 1. Finally, we need to test the usefulness of the observable resistance behaviour against our demystified fears. The fears are not what they were, so the resistance should change accordingly. With the worst fear cut down to size and even transformed into a Voice 2 creative place, the newly described resistance may look completely over the top. Asking the client to brainstorm a few optional actions which would be more effective for them in light of the reduced imaginings puts them, at least temporarily, into a Voice 2 activity which is positive and healthy. We have not made resistance a bad thing, we have only adjusted it to fit the revised threats.

Rabbits Out of a Hat: Transmogrification

Transmogrify. A swell word for changing something from one form to another. What if we could transmogrify a worst fear into a possibility? A nifty trick to be sure. Actually not a trick but a logical process.

Since we have defined worst fears as a production of mind, we can use the mind to transform that construct into possibility, another mental construct. What might follow, without further effort, is the exchange of an anxiety into release, and resistance behaviour into exploration. Additional completion of Voice 1, enrichment of Voice 2 and the shift of attention all in one move.

We can begin our transmogrification once we have done the rudimentary work to demystify the worst fears. We need to have cut these down to size, leaving some essential richness from our past that we do not want to lose. For example, suppose our team has a tradition of nimble interplay which has depended on a context of no defined roles and almost no definition of who has responsibility and authority for decision making. What success we've had has been due to everyone's ability to make it up in the moment and support everyone else. Now what has arrived is a new word, 'Governance'. And with that word come all kinds of role definition, specific authority and responsibilities for decision making and planning. One likely fear that can spring from this change is a worrisome loss of personal freedom, teamwork and performance. When it gets right down to it, everyone in the group has succeeded in the team because they really like to react in the moment, pick up any ball and move it along and at the end of the day be able to say, "We made it happen!" Now all that talent and skill suddenly seems to be of no value. It's projected to be written contracts, specific plans, rules, ring-fences and all the rest of stuff that feels like serious jail. Worst fear summary:

"Collaboration and teamwork are dead."

Time to put out our road warning signs that say "Danger, Transmogrifiers at work," and get started.

1. Discover and write down the values, or essence of what these folks believe they absolutely must carry forward into the future. It is pretty clear in our example that the essential values are collaboration and teamwork. We certainly want to get under those fuzzy words. But for now, let's take them at face value.
2. Identify what it is which seems to most threaten those values. In our example, what is the logic of Voice 1 which drives the threat to collaboration and teamwork? In this case it is the notion of 'governance.' So we need to get under that big word as well. Work on that reveals that the team is most threatened by the concept of 'single point authority.' Only one person will have the final say. No consensus, no democracy. No helping. Someone must deliver alone and has the final word, no matter how it has worked in the past.

3. Now comes the move of mind that can spring a new future. We move to the Possibility domain on the map and write both the essential historic values and the apparent threat next to each other. This is a claim on the future. Since we are standing squarely in possibility, we can claim that two things can coexist in the possibility, even though we don't yet see the details of how that is possible. So I claim that in a new, as yet unformed, world, our team can collaborate, be a satisfied team, have single point authority and be able to say, every day, at the end of the day, "we made this happen."

A curious thing occurs at this point. In order to pull this off, our language and tone changes from Voice 1 to Voice 2 and our minds move into creativity mode. The conversation turns to considering how this could be true, rather than how it cannot be true. Voice 1 does not disappear by any means. But a rational person has made a demand on the future that this collision of opposites, as seen from Voice 1, will be a synergy of talent and structure and process in the future, as seen from Voice 2 and lived out in Voice 3. This transformation gives Voice 1 immense comfort. The fear has done its work as the essence of it has been noted and carried forward, albeit in some new form. It's as if a gene structure has been assured new life in the future rather than lost to history. Voice 1 has done its work. The old forms can be laid to rest and energy turned to inventing the next form. Now our conversation can immediately turn to exploring the dimensions of the possibility and to some experiments which would reveal ways of enacting the possibility. So, we naturally complete Voice 1 and, just as naturally, find ourselves working in Voice 2.

Completing Reinvention

In the first phase, Voice 2 provides a holding place for the creative, exploratory urges we are experiencing in our transition. In the phase of completing the voices, Voice 2 is a place to reinvent the world. We push into the possibility without assessing probability.

We take small risks, experimenting with how things work in the world which are on our path but with which we have little or no experience. We do what we can to stimulate the feelings of lightness, openness and light-heartedness. We return to the world with the proverbial child's mind.

Completion takes time because we are exploring. Ideas form quickly at first. With exploration we get to feel, think and act our way into the possibilities, noticing how they fit and what they demand and deliver for us. Then a second wave of insight likely unfolds and is retested. In time, an energised form of the possibility becomes real to us. It may require some serious choice making or it forms cohesively, all ready to go.

Getting at the Learning Edge

The completion of the 'Possibility' domain occurs by exhausting what we-know-that-we-know and pushing into the unknown through intensive ideation. The ideation generates two general classes of material. First a rehash of existing thinking, even thinking that needs to end within this transition. Second, an underlying, emergent pattern among the idea sets which suggests new directions which need to be explored to reveal their promise for us.

When we have patterned the ideas we can test the patterns with our feelings. Touching on one from the note pad will spawn a feeling for each of us. If that pattern produces a feeling of greater release, lightens our load or, en-lightens us, then it is likely emergent. If it recalls the heaviness of Voice 1 then it is probably of our ending mental model. If neutral, it is probably something of business as usual which is continuing along without being much affected by the change at hand.

As we have seen, we can put apparently contradictory realities into the 'Possibility' domain with faith that we will find a new construct for the future by the collision of opposites. We may need to push these integrations way into the future so our smaller, tactical considerations do not defeat the synergy before it has started. When we have found a few emergent patterns and have defined those values and wisdoms from the past which we want to reinvent we are ready to evolve an integrated possibility which will require exploration. We ask ourselves how a world would look with every aspect of our desire served by and serving the others. How would a world be where synergy was the first order?

This is a conversation, rumination, query, and wander. As we hit on new integrations we continue using our witness to check the body sensations to tell us whether we are still in enlightening territory or have strayed into the left behind. Our goal is to follow our feelings and use our heads to stay at the positive, possible, emerging end of the work. And keep at it until something emergent becomes highly charged through our ventures of exploration and further ideation.

If I were the King, Queen or Emperor

Somewhere along the path of hanging out on the learning edge, our hands and feet get very itchy and want to get to work. While they have lots of known ways to go about building the future, those ways may be well rooted in an approach left over from the past. Just as we are finding emergent new frameworks of possibility for the future we also want to evolve physical methods which have some discovery built in. Our usual approach would be incremental: to build on what we know. That will not add to completion of Voice 2. But, if we were the King, the Queen or the Emperor – or any other person of unlimited power – we could just make it happen. By force of will, knowledge, money or charisma. So, we take our emergent possibility and ask ourself:

"If I were Emperor, what would I do to bring this possibility into reality?"

As with the possibility, we want to push this out over the edge, making it as bold as we can. For example, previously we spoke of a possibility where collaboration, teamwork and single point authority provided a profound synergy. We have thought about that some more, dug into the key words, kept asking for more and can now create it as a rich set of operating disciplines and skills we temporarily brand as a 'new way of working'. This hinges on some new, untried beliefs and considerable faith that we are as great as we think we are. We have a fabulous concept, but we have little idea of how it could actually work in the hands of human beings.

We ask ourselves, one by one, to play the Emperor/Picard/ Churchill or someone. And to make up a story about how they would proceed, right today, to bring our new collaborative/ authoritative approach about. This is another idea-generation process designed to get us out well past the boundaries of safety and into the unknown. Again, with some perseverance and time we will find emergent patterns in what we come up with as well as replays of the outworn. We can continue using the feelings test to find which is which and adjust aspects of the patterns to strengthen them.

In our example we discover that all roads lead to an unexpected strategy for action: a private space with a huge round table, like the court of King Arthur, with key roles and stakeholders present, but completely wired for all the new technical goodies. OK, we like it. All the feelings are on full takeoff power. What do we do next? We ask ourselves what we might try this week in a couple of hours' time for all of us to learn something about this approach, perhaps even trial it in a real meeting room with a real decision defining some measures of success which we can assess at the end of the week. And so on.

Rabbits Out of the Hat 2: Future Claims into Present Intention

So we have created this 'round table' notion as a new future for us. We've had a half dozen test runs with considerable adjustments to the concept and sense that the group is highly aligned. A couple of other competing schemes have arisen. The group is stuck now with a few really good options and need to test if they can get beyond Voice 2 which has dominated their concerns for a few weeks now.

Perhaps the option just chooses itself. The passion runs high, the time is right, the group has the authority to make it so and just moves ahead. Or there are choices and we need to close on a path by moving the essential, unyielding values, objectives and measures into the Voice 3 domain of 'Intention', allowing the feelings and actions to follow along. When we move the conversation to Voice 3, we are forcing it into hard numbers, real calendar time and specific investments and rewards. We do serious planning for each of our options, defining what it will take to bring our concept into what is really achievable with real resources. Then we test our passion, the feelings in Voice 3. We will be most resolved and energised in one of them. Or none will emerge and we must return to do more choice creation work in Voice 2.

Making the turn between Voice 2 and Voice 3 is a dance. We go over the line and back and over again. Remember we are still doing completion work in Voice 2. We are play-acting Voice 3 as a way of extended exploration. We agree to turn off Voice 2 and speak in Voice 3 long enough to learn how pragmatic our options are. The turning point is found in the rise of a real passion to succeed. In Voice 2, the feelings are about lightness. So we can say, "That would be cool!" Yes, it is a nifty idea, a neat possibility. That is not resolute, fervent passion to transform that possibility into an important reality. The shift in the tone of the feelings signals the turn to Voice 3 as we move over and back in our testing.

Completing the Commitment

The ending has ended, the reinvention has been accomplished and the way forward is clear for a while. We have arrived in Voice 3, in a whole-hearted embrace of a new construct of objectives, plans and commitment. We don't use the TransforMAP solely for Voice 3. Voice 3 is the predominant structure of working and project management in our familiar world. There are a zillion books and schools and experts to teach us all about every part of it.

Voice 3 is so dominant in our culture that the other two

voices are seen as parts of it. The Voice 1 / Voice 2 creativity of the designer is seen as a discipline within Voice 3. The artist, living in Voice 2, is not recognised in business thinking except as a resource for Voice 3 activity – creating physical works which can become monetary value through a commercial path. In the main, in this time of the world, the global business culture sees the sole, valuable agenda for all of us to be growth targets and disciplined achievement based on fervent commitment to creating shareholder value by gaining and retaining power in the marketplace and exploiting that power. From this strategic view, human change is another challenge to be gotten through on the path. When we talk business, we need to be able to talk in Voice 3.

Of course, good business people know that change is pretty constant, uncertainty runs high, the motive and alignment of the employee base is all over the map, technological and social surprises come faster and faster and just about the time we get something important into Voice 3 action, the goal posts move. So we never seem to really complete anything. If we attempt to operate in a system completely defined in Voice 3, we know where it leads: it goes all pear-shaped once again when the world has moved and we have moved and the new construct has run its course and the disciplines begin to fail, the intentions seem out of date, fervour gives way to complacency and safety and the stock price is sinking. Then, the intentions and disciplines and feelings of Voice 3 will transmogrify into another Voice 1 and no matter what we call it, we will be off on another cycle of ending, reinvention and commitment.

Given my point of view, I choose to define the completion of Voice 3 as a process of exhausting what we know until we can identify the first point at which something in our new scheme will have to end. And where our disciplines are really temporary and must be reinvented and how our best intention will likely change halfway through the schedule because of changes in the world. In other words, completion of Voice 3 leads to the reality of another Voice 1, just around the corner.

Many people still see transition as a temporary state. We

unfreeze things, change them and then re-freeze. I think we could look at the world like that in the 1950s. But surely no more. Exhausting Voice 3 is making what we can of it in the time we have before the game changes at its root. Voice 3 is just as much a temporary, moving condition as Voices 1 and 2.

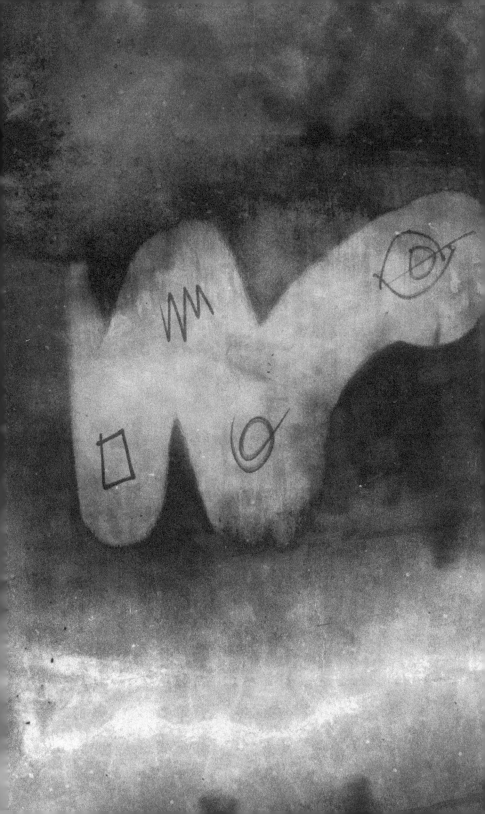

The Path Ahead

Each of the maps and frameworks in the second part of this book prompts a conversation that is bigger than the known limits of the client and ourselves, conducted in an essentially boundless mind space you will learn to create. Each has its place, contributing something distinctive to the much larger transformational journey.

These maps have been decades in the making and have formed the basis for a flourishing practice for me and a small number of colleagues. Their secrets have been kept under corporate wraps for thirty years, accessible only under tight licensing conditions. But I now wish to offer much wider access to this material and to the philosophy and thinking that underpins it.

Because it is clear to me that the family of life can little afford to have the human system continue stalling when faced with change and uncertainty. Most anywhere we look we see things coming apart at the seams. It is a time of unparalleled opportunity to dig in and transform the world to a more sustainable, liveable place for everything and everybody. The design opportunity of all time, literally. I believe these maps can help.

Through the elegant infrastructure established by my friends at Executive Arts you can now access more exploratory essays, case studies, workshop materials, coaching, professional training, a suite of apps, and other resources relating to the core maps – alongside some of the smartest and most experienced practitioners in the business.

It has also been gratifying to see International Futures Forum take these maps up as a critical element in their practice of transformative innovation and system transition, integrating them alongside the Three Horizons framework as a cornerstone in their programmes for developing the 21st-century competencies for making a difference and living well in today's world.

From the earliest years of starting to explore this work I had a fuzzy but passionate idea of being of service to others. I wanted to teach. My calling to master the work was to see to it that people got better chances to live out the best expression of themselves and that I would teach others to continue the work.

In the late 1980s, I spoke my passion one evening over noodles at the Hunan Empire Restaurant, just off Union Street in San Francisco, with three of my dearest buddies, David Sibbet, Joan McIntosh and Lenny Lind. We were trading stories about our passions for making a difference and the meaning in our lives. When it was my turn, this came out of me: "My path is to make sure that whoever I journey with has the best chance to fully express who they can be and become."

I offer this book and the core suite of transition maps it introduces in fulfilment of that pledge.

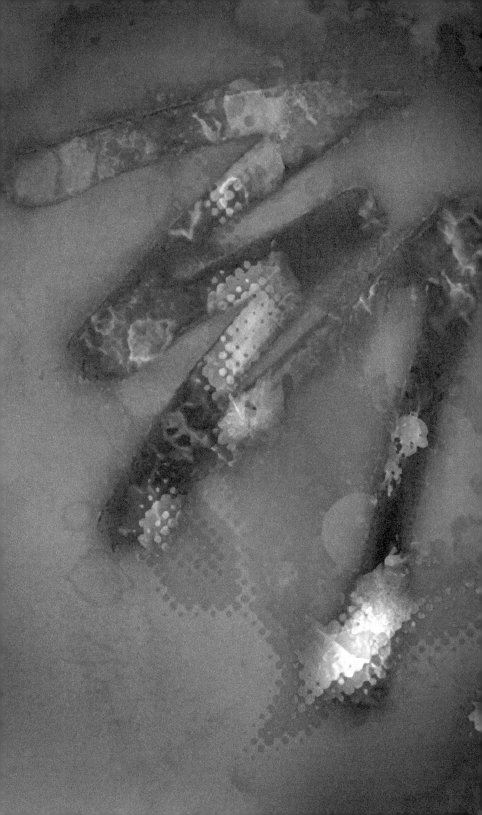

Appendix: A Brief History of the TransforMAP

I include here as a postscript this brief history of TransforMAP. I do so partly to name and honour some of the many sources who have inspired my work over decades, but also to make transparent the serendipitous design process that has produced the current version of the map. It's been a long, patient road and I have stood on some strong shoulders of therapists and writers along the way. Any of their work makes good reading.

Elisabeth Kübler-Ross

The first work came from Elisabeth Kübler-Ross. *On Death and Dying* is her 1969 seminal observation of five stages of human progression through our last days.

She opened a wide door for examining the process of human death – a conversation taboo in American culture then and even now.

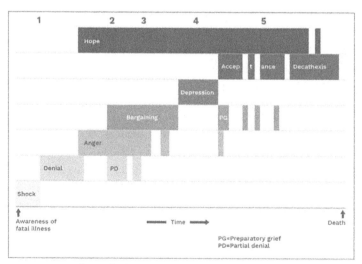

Source: "Stages" of Dying - Elisabeth Kübler-Ross Foundation

Her diagram fascinated me, because it contains two stellar notions. First, there is a mighty transformation at the end. Like a butterfly emerging from its cocoon, we shed all vestiges of our prior existence as we will soon shed our body and live however briefly in a transcendent state. Engineer that I was at the time, the question I took away was, "How the hell does that work?"

Second, and no less compelling, the bliss state, if you will, co-exists in time with the trauma of our mind getting to grips with the reality that it will soon have no host body to fuel it and carry it around. We are doing both dances at once.

Many conversations later, these two notions became clearer and are embedded in the TransforMAP.

Stanley Keleman

In 1974 Stanley Keleman published Living Your Dying, a call to use the many 'little deaths' we suffer – losing loved ones, jobs, our health, the car keys, the prowess of youth, and so on – to prepare ourselves for our 'big death', the end of our physical existence.

If you or someone close to you is facing their own end, take some time and read this book to them. Keleman deftly moves us away from the myths of dying promulgated by our culture toward a direct experience of each moment. Elegant work.

In my early thirties I was not interested in the physical dying. At seventy-four (as I write this) he is speaking right at me. What was of immense value at the time was the notion of a turning point. Keleman introduced a profound idea which stuck with me.

> "Important events occur in everyone's life that are the focus of new directions. These turning points signal that one way of living is over and a new way is emerging; they are the rites of passage in a life.... Turning points are emotional journeys. They are life's upswellings. They are the intersections and intensifications of new encounters, new images, new impulses, catalysing, brewing riches, charging the atmosphere. They are the roots of new directions and self-formation. They are the shapers of our bodies."

One of the joys of reading Keleman is to find the lyrics and the music in his writing.

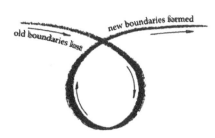

The turning point I was interested in was the move from angst, worst fears and avoidance into the transcendent, joyful freedom to embark on the next stage of discovery. But I need to back up just a bit in the story to give us all the pieces and parts for the new construction I was about to draw.

Roger Gould

In the mid-seventies I partnered with Roger Gould, a psychiatrist from Los Angeles. Together we designed executive workshops and a weekend experience for referrals to Roger's practice. Roger's mantra was, "You aren't sick, you are just changing". His fine book, *Transformations,* is the study of male adult ageing and staging. While it became a pretty stormy relationship, I'll always be grateful to Roger for how available he was with his work. I took away a couple of gems which find their way into much of my own work.

First, new energies are always stirring inside ourselves. They want to be heard and recognised and nurtured and grow to be an actor on our stage. Call it an emerging talent or quality. Perhaps it is latent and is called forth in our life circumstances. Perhaps it was just dropped into our unconscious realms by the Force. Probably both. No matter, something is always emerging.

If left un-addressed, the energy becomes disruptive, we may feel victimised by it, and if suppressed it may make us sick, and in the extreme, kill us. In our workshops we sought to give voice to these emerging qualities, by providing a protected place to explore them, with air and light and time. We midwifed the renegotiation of the self to integrate the birth of this fledgling entity with the rest of the powers that were.

The second gem I received was a look at what goes on as we attempt to bring the emergent voices into our conscious view. I've called this the learning edge. When we make the slightest move into action with the emergent energy, our body can react emotionally with a set of sensations which warn us mightily not to go there.

For example, in my own experience I used to talk about my plan to leave engineering and take up this new career doing change work. For a year, whenever I started talking, I had about five minutes before my throat felt like I'd been hit hard in the neck. I could barely wheeze out any words.

Once those sensations start raging, our heads imagine a nightmare of awful things. We try avoiding the pain by pulling in our horns and backing away from the edge to safer ground. Roger went to work testing all the fear, uncertainty and doubt in our heads, cutting the demons down to size.

I saw people go through a turning point as Gould worked to demystify the demons. And once through, as in Kübler-Ross's work, they moved to a new perspective. From being held back and stuck, into a positive, innovative attitude as they re-invented and renegotiated their lives.

Between Kübler-Ross, Gould and Keleman, I could draw a new picture.

 After struggling on the edge, doing the work to finish the past and open the door to a new future, we would swing through the turning point, shedding the outworn stuff of our lives, heading into a transformed, albeit uncertain, personhood.

I shared this story widely. One day a hand went up with a question. It was from an Italian. He suggested that my drawing and the story seemed so Northern European, so cold and so dark, that he was put off. I could not disagree. What could I do, he asked, to put some heart and hope into this dreary slog into despair and back?

In one of my finer improvisational moments, I turned the drawing on its head, he being Italian and all, and told the story all over again as a climb towards an ideal.

As we climbed we had to put down more and more baggage. The higher we climbed the closer we got to our deeper purposes, our dreams, our ultimate possibility. At the very top, we had no kinetic energy, but immense potential if we just took one step onward. With that step we accelerated through another turning point into a new focused life. It was a great performance if I do say so myself. The crowd got high on it as did I. So I kept it in the act. Two pictures of the territory, two ways to describe the journey. But even with these maps, I didn't have conversations or tools, only descriptions of the territory.

A friend visited one day and I did a proud show and tell of both stories. He offered that for him the down and dark story preceded the up and light story. They were really connected. Lights went on. Damn. Where had I been? The output of one was the input to the next. I was thrilled because it seemed undeniably true. And humbled because I had not seen that relationship earlier.

His insight was the key to what became the TransforMAP as a description of the territory, almost thirty years on. But we aren't there yet, there was more to be revealed.

This 'more' had to wait until I encountered Voice Dialogue.

Hal and Sidra Stone

Hal Stone was a Jungian psychologist, artist, and leader. It was my good fortune to know, travel and learn with Hal and his wife Sidra when Hal was head of the Center for the Healing Arts in Los Angeles.

Hal and Sidra pioneered the art of the voice dialogue – engaging sub-personalities in dialogues of discovery. While most therapists still were looking for a well-integrated personality, Hal observed and worked with inner characters possessed of their own agendas, voices and complexities.

In 1989, Hal and Sidra summarised thirty years of their work in their book Embracing Our Selves. If you hope to master the practice I describe in these pages, Hal and Sidra are a required read.

Hal and Sidra did not see Voice Dialogue as an 'it'; rather an adjunct to otherwise good training. People have borrowed freely from their insights. I am one of those fortunate to do so. Hal and Sidra's work goes deep and has immense range.

I use just the idea that since our amazing mind constantly presents our waking awareness with a seamless picture of the world, we can always define a voice we would like to speak with or listen to. Our deeper mind will then conjure it into existence from somewhere within ourselves, a working facsimile of the personality or the voice that we have asked for.

Roberto Assagioli

In 1974, Roberto Assagioli, an Italian psychotherapist, wrote The Act of Will. From the Frontispiece:

> *"Roberto Assagioli is one of the masters of modern psychology in the line that runs from Sigmund Freud through C.G. Jung and Abraham Maslow. Himself, a colleague of all these men, he was among the pioneers of psychoanalysis in Italy, though he pointed out that Freud had largely neglected the higher reaches of human nature. Over the years Dr. Assagioli has developed a comprehensive psychology known as psychosynthesis. Psychosynthesis sees man as tending naturally toward harmony within himself and with the world. Dr. Assagioli's concept of the will is a key part of that vision."*

Psychosynthesis envisions our personality as a collection of sub-personalities who come on and off stage as necessary to get us along in life. There is a very big cast of characters, but a handful seem to be dominant players at any one time. The Will is the stage director who can woo, cajole, and lead the many voices to play nice and be on and offstage as required to make life work. Our Will has volition, making truly new choices, where the sub-personalities seem stuck in habitual patterns.

If this sounds like an entrée to voice dialogue – between this cast of sub-personalities – it is exactly that.

Pierro Ferrucci

Pierro Ferrucci was a student and colleague of Assagioli. *What We May Be* is a marvellous workbook, offering guided imagery experiences to meet and mature the 'baby' sub-personalities. As if parenting recalcitrant teens, Ferrucci takes them on learning journeys to build a creative relationship with the Will/stage manager, and to improve their perspective on one another. In and of itself it is a powerful therapy.

I offer this sweet, telling excerpt from his book:

> *"Inner dialogue is suited for all occasions, but it is particularly useful in certain special moments, such as when:*
>
> *We are facing an important choice*
>
> *We are in crisis*
>
> *We think that nobody understands us*
>
> *We want to tap our inner wisdom*
>
> *We feel lonely*
>
> *We are ready for a change*
>
> *We want a free session*
>
> *But the effects of inner dialogue can go well beyond the unblocking of an impasse...*
>
> *...We can learn how to rely on our Self rather than*

> *following the pressures of other people or of our own sub-personalities. We can discover how to take the whole situation into account instead of being influenced by intense but unimportant elements. There is also the possibility of finding that the solution of a problem can always be found at a level higher than the one where the problem itself lies. Moreover, we can avoid all the complications that follow decisions made in a superficial, hurried, heedless way."*

By now this should sound quite familiar. Ferrucci makes Assagioli's work very accessible.

With Hal, Roberto and Pierro on my side, I grasped the sense of a sub-personality with feelings, a logical component and the ability to act out in the physical world. And groups of these varied characters on stage together.

I appreciated what was happening when someone, confronted with a new situation, could be excited by it and be speaking the word "Yes", while their head rotated side to side, saying "no", while they perspired and turned a new shade of red, and their feet tried to get them out of the room.

It became possible to have a conversation with the feet, or the perspiration, or the person who was completely up for the journey or the head saying no.

All of which, you will now see, led to the full version of the TransforMAP as you see it today, with the two loops, the three 'voices' and the three domains of heart, head and feet.

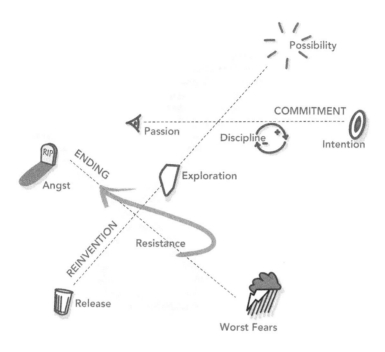

About this Book

About the Author

In 1979 Jim Ewing committed himself to working on his inner passion: facilitating individuals who were striving to express their talents and commitments as fully as possible. After a dozen years of rocket science, Jim abandoned his engineering roots to learn all he could about Transactional Analysis, Gestalt Therapy, Psychodrama, Voice Dialogue, and adult aging and staging.

Each of the maps that Jim developed is based on the core insight that creative motion on the path of learning, design and transformation begins with hints, clues, guesses, slips of the tongue, unknowing and making it up. In other words, in the shadows rather than in the known. Each provides a process for generating such material and for capturing it in a way which is later transformed to reveal patterns which open the door to discovery and creative testing. The disciplines require both spatial and linear thinking in equal measure, calling on the whole person, and are most powerful when taken as a learning path to a different insight about the world.

Jim passed away in 2014 after a period of illness throughout which he remained a positive and inspiring presence to all who knew him. His wish was that his work would continue beyond him, and we hope that he would be thrilled to see us making his wisdom accessible to a world so clearly in need of it.

About Executive Arts

The 'Executive' in Executive Arts refers to the character within each of us who has the ability to choose a new path for our self. In industry it is at the executive level that strategic decisions are formed, made and directed. Good executives are called on to break corporate habits, take a bet on new technology or markets, restructure and inspire their population of managers and workers to abandon some, or much, of what they know and set off on an uncertain course. The executive within must be capable of managing the inner call to a new direction, directing the unlearning and learning, and redesigning from an 'idea' through to 'possibility' and on to 'achievement'. This is an art more than a science. Hence Executive Arts.

The Executive Arts embrace learning, design and transformation as one energising process rather than three separate elements in a commonly compartmentalised world.

Part of Jim Ewing's vision for his work was that the maps he had developed would be stewarded and cared for by a dedicated 'circle' of expert practitioners: Patrick Heneghan, Pamela Deans, Alan Russell, Graham Leicester, Mark Denton, Mike Heneghan, and Frank Crawford.

Circles of people have been a powerful form over the course of history. Traditionally they have represented strength and power, built for protection, invention, manifestation or healing. They are marvellous structures. Everyone can see everyone else without hierarchy or rank limiting the view. Circles expand and contract without reorganisation. Anyone can sit anywhere and partner with anyone else. Circles define a commons for holding all we share.

To learn more about Executive Arts and the support it can offer in using Jim's maps and frameworks, please visit:

www.executivearts.co.uk

About IFF

IFF is a charity registered in Scotland with a mission to enable people and organisations to flourish as effective agents in powerful times. We work with governments, communities, businesses, foundations and individuals. We address complex, messy, seemingly intractable issues – local, global and all levels in between – fostering practical hope and wise initiative. We support people making a difference in the face of all that stands in the way of making a difference, rising to the challenge of the moment. We develop their 21st-century competencies for thriving in complexity and their capacity for inspiring and transformative innovation. We offer resources to support this activity through a thriving community Hub, events, workshops, tools, processes, training and other online materials available in the IFF Practice Centre.

www.internationalfuturesforum.com

About Triarchy Press

Triarchy Press is an independent publisher of books that bring a systemic or contextual approach to many areas of life, including:

Government, Education, Health and other public services ~ Ecology and Regenerative Cultures ~ Leading and Managing Organizations ~ The Money System ~ Psychotherapy and other Expressive Therapies ~ Walking, Psychogeography and Mythogeography ~ Movement and Somatics ~ Innovation ~ The Future and Future Studies

For books by Nora Bateson, Daniel Wahl, Russ Ackoff, Barry Oshry, John Seddon, Phil Smith, Bill Tate, Patricia Lustig, Sandra Reeve, Graham Leicester, Nelisha Wickremasinghe, Gregory Bateson, Bill Sharpe, Alyson Hallett, Lucy Neal, Miranda Tufnell and other remarkable writers, please visit:

www.triarchypress.net